Family Therapy

Family therapy is increasingly recognised as one of the evidence based psychotherapies. In contemporary therapeutic practice, family therapy is helpful across the age span and for distress caused by family conflict, trauma and mental health difficulties. Because of this, many psychotherapists integrate elements of family therapy within their approaches.

Family Therapy: 100 Key Points and Techniques provides a concise and jargon-free guide to 100 of the fundamental ideas and techniques of this approach.

Divided into helpful sections, it covers:

* Family therapy theory
* Essential family therapy practice
* Using family therapy techniques
* Common challenges in family therapy
* Contemporary debates and issues
* Self issues for family therapists.

Family Therapy: 100 Key Points and Techniques is an invaluable resource for psychotherapists and counsellors in training and in practice. As well as appealing to established family therapists, this latest addition to the 100 Key Points series will also find an audience with other mental health professionals working with families and interested in learning more about family therapy techniques.

Mark Rivett is a UKCP registered family therapist and Senior Lecturer and Director of Family Therapy Training at Bristol University. He is the current editor of the *Journal of Family Therapy*.

Eddy Street is a Chartered Clinical and Counselling Psychologist (BPS) and having spent most of his professional career in NHS Child and Adolescent Mental Health Services he is now working independently. He is a past editor of the *Journal of Family Therapy*, and has published widely on this subject.

100 Key Points

Series Editor: Windy Dryden

ALSO IN THIS SERIES:

Cognitive Therapy: 100 Key Points and Techniques
Michael Neenan and Windy Dryden

Rational Emotive Behaviour Therapy: 100 Key Points and Techniques
Windy Dryden and Michael Neenan

Family Therapy

100 key points and techniques

*Mark Rivett and
Eddy Street*

Routledge
Taylor & Francis Group

LONDON AND NEW YORK

First published 2009
by Routledge
27 Church Road, Hove, East Sussex BN3 2FA

Simultaneously published in the USA and Canada
by Routledge
711 Third Avenue, New York NY1007 (8th Floor)

Routledge is an imprint of the Taylor & Francis Group, an Informa
business

Typeset in Times by Garfield Morgan, Swansea, West Glamorgan

Paperback cover design by Andrew Ward

This publication has been produced with paper manufactured to
strict environmental standards and with pulp derived from
sustainable forests.

British Library Cataloguing in Publication Data
A catalogue record for this book is available from the British Library

Library of Congress Cataloging-in-Publication Data
Rivett, Mark.
   Family therapy : 100 key points and techniques / Mark Rivett &
Eddy Street.
        p. ; cm. (100 key points)
   ISBN 978-0-415-41038-0 (hbk.) ISBN 978-0-415-41039-7 (pbk.)
1. Family psychotherapy. I. Street, Eddy. II. Title. III. Series: 100 key
points.
   [DNLM: 1. Family Therapy–methods. WM 430.5.F2 R624f 2009]
   RC488.5.R586 2009
   616.89'156–dc22

                                              2009003867

ISBN: 978-0-415-41038-0 (hbk)
ISBN: 978-0-415-41039-7 (pbk)

To Leonard who would have told me
which were the best points

and

With heartfelt gratitude to all my teachers

Contents

Preface

Family therapy has always believed itself to be the most radical and innovative of the 'mainstream' psychotherapies. This is because, at its core, it asserts that all problems experienced by human beings have an interactional component. Sometimes, family therapists even talk about the 'self' as consisting of a web of relationships and interpretations of those relationships rather than a 'core' and 'solid' phenomenon. Family therapy argues that because of these aspects of human existence the solution to human problems requires attention to the interactional space: the space *between* people not *within* them.

Some 'folk' axioms support such a view: 'No problem is an orphan' (an Albanian saying provided by Rainela Xhmollari) or 'It is the people we love who keep us the way we are'. In a nutshell, this is the paradox of family therapy and its most precious gift to the therapeutic world: Relationships are constituents of problems and only by working with relationships can these problems be healed. To paraphrase Philip Larkin (1974), families may 'f. . . you up' (Larkin 1974) but no full resolution can be achieved without the help of the family. What family therapy adds to this insight is that such relationship work is best undertaken with these relationships *in the therapeutic room itself* rather than reported second hand in the therapeutic encounter. It is from this perspective that family therapists have created specific techniques to work with family groups and couples.

These ideas have motivated family therapists from the pioneering days of the 1960s to the more sedate, professional era of the 2000s. In contemporary therapeutic discourse, it is common to support your therapy with research findings and they are indeed now impressive for family therapy. This form of therapy is recommended by governmental and scientific professional bodies for childhood difficulties (Sprenkle 2002; NICE 2004a, 2004c, 2004d, 2005), eating disorders (NICE 2004b), substance misuse (Rowe and Liddle 2002) and adult mental health difficulties (Jones and Asen 2000), to name just a few (see Carr 2009a and 2009b for a fuller description).

This book will explain the fundamental key ideas and techniques of family therapy by adopting the '100 points' model. Adapting to this model has been challenging for us in many ways. We have clearly had to restrict our choice of points. When we set out we had the vain hope that we could encapsulate the craft of family therapy in 100 key points. Fortunately, life is not like that. We have had to balance what we think is 'key' (and argued about it) in both practical and theoretical senses. Inevitably, some of the intense theoretical debate that has consumed the field, we have had to restrict. This is largely because this book is more of a 'how to' manual, rather than a theoretical elaboration (see Rivett and Street 2003 for a fuller discussion of these). We have equally decided to seek a tone that reflects this 'how to' text: neither too academic nor too journalistic. This has had its inevitable complexities. Apart from finding a way of describing patterns of therapeutic behaviour that for both of us span almost 30 years, the task has made us describe one technique succinctly when others have written whole books on that self same technique.

We hope that we have managed to balance these aspects of the task by allowing ourselves a more 'academic' tone in some points while in others we have retained a practical focus. Accordingly, this book can be read 'out of sequence' with no difficulty: the book maintains what is clearly a false division between theoretical and practical points. Parts 2, 10 and 11 are largely theoretical. In these parts we cover some of the debates about systems theory and family therapy (Part 2), the wider context for the practising of family therapy (Part 10) and general professional themes (Part 11). Parts 3, 4 and 5 on the other hand contain the 'core' family therapy skills, including how to set the context for family therapy (Part 3), and generic family therapy techniques (Parts 4 and 5). Part 6 describes specific techniques that have their origins in particular 'branches' or 'schools' of family therapy. There are a series of case examples in these sections of the book and all such examples are composite vignettes rather than 'real' families. Because family therapy is a therapeutic craft, in Parts 8 and 9 we have concentrated on points related to the self of the therapist and on problems encountered in family therapy. We wanted to ensure in this broad collection of points that family therapy with its systemic practice component is *more than* a collection of techniques: It is a world view.

In some senses, writing this book has also forced us to review what we see as the 'basic' skills of the family therapist. This has been informed by both our practice, in which we need to explain to families why we do what we do, and also by teaching family therapy to many kinds of students. What we have therefore written is a series of points that vary in length and detail and cover the separate stages of family therapy treatment. Clearly, the result is our own view and may not reflect those of our professional colleagues but we hope it does reflect some core techniques and concepts that all family therapists would value. These colleagues would notice for instance that we do not specifically highlight the 'Milan' school of family therapy in Part 6. This is because we believe that Milan ideas and techniques are a bedrock from which many of the other techniques flow.

As a short introduction to family therapy, this book is designed to help students of family therapy learn about the approach but it is also designed as a book that will explain family therapy to therapists of other hues and in other trainings. It also will have value to other professions within the human services sector: social workers, nurses, psychologists, GPs, psychiatrists, organisational consultants. We hope that we have produced a pragmatic introduction to one of the most vibrant and challenging psychotherapies of the time.

Mark Rivett and Eddy Street

Part 1

SYSTEMS THEORY

1

What is a system?

The fundamental theory that underlies the interactional 'mind set' of family therapists is that of systems theory (Bateson 1972, 1979; Nichols and Schwartz 1998; Becvar and Becvar 1999; Glick *et al.* 2000; Goldenberg and Goldenberg 2000; Dallos and Draper 2005). For instance, Walrond-Skinner (1976) called family therapy 'the treatment of natural systems'. This is the radical root of all the ideas and techniques that grow within the 'tradition' of family therapy. Indeed, many family therapists prefer to be called 'systemic therapist' rather than 'family therapist'. So naturally, this is where *Family Therapy: 100 Key Points and Techniques* must start.

It is not possible to conceive of the functioning of the natural world without thinking in terms of the operation of systems. Let us take a simple natural process in a particular location: In any field the plants and animals are linked to each other in terms of their habitats and the climate they inhabit. They form an ecological 'system'. Their interdependence is demonstrated when an unusually hot summer occurs. For instance, the heightened temperature causes an increase in the number of insects living in the field and this results in more birds visiting the field looking for food. However, let us say that the increased number of birds destroys some of the plants on which the insects live. So now the field becomes a less favourable habitat for the insects and their number decreases. Before long the birds too decrease as they go elsewhere looking for insects to eat. The natural world is full of such ecological systems.

We can consider the field and its inhabitants as a system but it would not be helpful to think that this system is separate from the rest of the world. The hedge around the field does not seal this ecological system 'in', but is an arbitrary way in which we define the system we are studying. For example we might focus down on one corner of the field that retains moisture more easily than others. Hence in this small 'subsystem' of the field different plants may grow, which in turn support different insects. These may attract different birds. Thus we have defined a new smaller system within the larger ecosystem of the field. Similarly we can expand our view of the field to include other fields in the locality. This will give us a wider picture of flora and wildlife activity in the context of many fields. Our field then becomes a 'subsystem' of the locality. One way of describing this is to say that everything is potentially a subsystem of something else. The process by which we determine which system we will arbitrarily look at is called, by family therapists, *punctuating the system*.

There are other dimensions to consider when thinking about natural systems. All systems move through time. Thus, we might think about how human cultivation affected the ecology of the field, and we might also think about the effects of global warming on our field. The *boundary* and *punctuation* that we adopt when we look at a system therefore might be defined by geography, time or *what determines our intention/focus* (in other words the context of the 'observer'). Systems theory implies that all systems are permeable (their boundaries are loose), that what is inside and outside any system is an arbitrary act of definition and that any system can be viewed from a multitude of 'lenses'. Bateson (Bateson and Bateson 1988) and some family therapists (Keeney 1983) have argued that no one can ever fully describe any system: Descriptions are partial and biased by the intention/ prejudices of the describer (Keeney 1983; Cecchin and Lane 1991). The recognition that the observer influences what is observed has been called *second order systems theory or second order cybernetics* (Becvar and Becvar 1999). Thus a human being observing the field may scare off a substantial number of birds, so the bird population cannot be accurately measured: The observer system is a skewed version of the non-observed system.

To return to the field: It is possible to identify characteristics of naturally occurring systems by highlighting the way in which the 'parts' are interrelated and interact each with the other. These multiple interrelations influence the system's total functioning. We can therefore consider the functioning of the system in terms of the patterns of connection between the parts. This is why many systems theorists claim that 'the whole is greater than the sum of its parts'. These connections involve the exchange of information. In our field, this information exchange is about plants growing with the increase in temperature, insects eating plants, birds eating insects, etc. Each part connects to, and interrelates in some way with, the other parts and what occurs in this information exchange will depend on the nature of the system. This process of information exchange is called *feedback*. In the field more plants might lead to more insects, which will lead to more birds. This is called *escalating/reinforcing feedback* (O'Connor and McDermott 1997). Alternatively, the feedback might 'halt' the pattern and cause a decrease in the original process. In the field this will occur when the plant population declines. This kind of feedback is called *balancing feedback* (O'Connor and McDermott 1997). Within human systems information exchange can occur via words, feelings and behavioural interaction.

Systems typically use the information that passes between the constituent parts to attempt to maintain itself in a balance. A change in one element will produce new information that will be communicated, resulting in a change elsewhere in the system so that functioning is not effected. An example is the way the human body maintains its temperature by causing us to sweat or take off clothes when we are hot. In systems theory, this process is called *homeostasis*. However, because all systems are to some extent open to outside influence, which is uncontrollable by them, and because systems evolve (move through time), they also constantly change. This process is called *morphogenesis* in systems theory.

2

The family as a system

Family therapists are interested in applying systems theory to families whatever their structure may be, e.g. 'nuclear' families, gay and lesbian families, lone parent families, step-families and extended families (Walrond-Skinner 1976; Nock 2000; McGoldrick and Hardy 2008). Accordingly, the focus of family therapists is on the pattern of connections between one individual and another, each component of a family system being seen as contributing to its operation as a whole.

In the same way that in a natural system a change in one part has an effect on another part, this also occurs in families, with every behaviour having a relationship dynamic. A simple family example would be noting how the way a mother and father interact has an impact on how one of them deals with their child's behaviour. This in turn will produce feedback, which may or may not change the way the parents interact. Of course the process of feedback makes for complex processes. For instance the child may then provide differential feedback to each parent, which may lead to an escalating pattern. Therefore the family functions by means of patterns of connections between its members. These connections are established by the process of information exchange (emotional, cognitive or behavioural), which constitutes communication.

Within families the usual way of exchanging information may initially appear to be by verbal communication but we also have to consider non-verbal communication and all the other ways in which people behave. In a family it is *impossible not to communicate*: Everything that any one person does provides an opportunity for information exchange within and between family members. As an open human system the family can therefore be considered to be defined by its communicational patterns. These often provide the 'definition' of the family in phrases such as 'we are a close family', 'Dad is closer to his daughter than his son', etc. These definitions (note they are always 'partial' in any systemic interpretation) provide the 'meaning' of the 'family' to its members. It is also important to recognise that some communication is contradictory. This concept was termed *the double bind* by Bateson (1972). Thus, the child in the above example may say he is angry with his mother but may behave lovingly by, for instance, asking for a cuddle from her. Bateson believed that such contradictory patterns of communication were unhelpful. He also described relationship patterns in which behaviours centred around escalating feedback (he called these *symmetrical* relationships) and complementary feedback (*complementary* relationships). If the father for instance became aggressive with his child, in our example, the relationship would be symmetrical if the child responded with aggression too. If however the child became compliant, the relationship would be complementary.

The capacity to see families not as a collection of individual 'selves' but as a gestalt, a whole, leads to a crucial aspect of systems theory and family therapy practice. Individual characteristics in family members are seen as behavioural forms of communication rather than as personal attributes located within an individual. From this perspective it is more accurate to describe individuals as communicating certain behaviours rather than describing them as being a particular type of person. Therefore, to say that someone is a controlling person does not capture the sense of all the interactions around that person at any particular time. Nor does it include (as a systemic description) the perspective of the describer, who may only be offering a partial definition of that person because of their own position in the system. It is more accurate to report that when certain interactions occur within the family's communicational system then that person is displaying 'controlling type' behaviour. Human action and activity are therefore embedded within the connections, the interactions, between people.

Information exchange, what we have termed 'communication', is the fuel of the interaction in human systems. To be human is to communicate and to communicate is to be in relation to someone else. Indeed, from this perspective, it is not so much that an individual 'communicates' as it is that the individual is constituted by his or her communication. The process of communication in terms of its frequency and impact is what determines the boundaries of the family system. Individuals who live together and share intimate moments and tasks such as childcare, caring for the elderly, financial budgets, etc. have a continual stream of communication that contributes to the definition of who they are. With our example above a grandparent might be involved in caring for the child when the child is ill. This person has less communication overall than the other members but at particular times he/she will have a significant impact on what happens and therefore the boundaries of the family have some fluidity and at any particular moment will depend on who is considered to be involved and with whom. Families therefore also have subsystems in the same way that other natural systems have. In this sense the boundary of any family or human system is dependent on how the individuals themselves wish to define it or how external observers wish to define who is in and who is out of that system. Individuals are therefore part of the communication system we call the family and to be involved in a communication system continually is at the core of human identity.

3

Individuals and systems

Even though humans are social creatures embedded as we have implied in families, groups and cultures, all of which are systems, there is a twist in the systemic nature of the individual person. We all become blinded to the systemic nature of being a human being. Even though we are always part of something else, we somehow forget it.

This is because every behaviour is at one and the same time both an expression of that person and a communication to others. To emphasise one to the neglect of the other is to lose our essential systemic nature. Yet for us as individuals there is a strong tendency to experience our communications solely as expressions of the self. We emphasise the 'what I do' to the neglect of 'this is my contribution to what we do'.

Another reason why human beings lose an overall conception of their systemic nature is that they need to formulate action ahead of events; they need to create strategies and tactics prior to being involved in situations of informational complexity. In constructing our own stories or narratives of what has happened in the past (or what will happen in the future) we make a reflexive withdrawal from ongoing events; we stand outside of what is happening at that moment and give ourselves space to 'think'. The individual then focuses on a self-conscious view rather than on the consciousness of the moment where the ongoing activities of others will have important influences on the interactive process. Doing this allows us to work out what we are going to do but the 'timeout' period results in a loss of awareness of how the system is operating. The degree to which any individual indulges in an overly focused view of his or her own particular conception of events in the system will determine the extent to which that person is distant from appreciating his or her operation within the functioning system. Within families this happens continually as family members focus on 'this is what I need', or 'this is what others do to me', rather than considering the process of interaction for the family as a whole. Individuals and families therefore have the ability to understand the social interactive nature of themselves but unfortunately this understanding requires the individual to subsume his or her view within that of the system and it does not occur readily, particularly at times when problems arise.

The idea that human beings find systemic thinking unnatural suggests that family therapy is constantly in tension with many other 'individually' orientated therapies. Most helping services are designed to 'blame' one family member and seek to organise, change or ameliorate that person's behaviour, beliefs or feelings. For this reason early family therapists (Haley 1981) warned *against* family therapy becoming part of mental health services. Contrary to many such approaches to therapy, family therapy always places individuals' beliefs, behaviours and emotions in *context*. In doing so, it either dilutes blame or seeks to escape blaming interventions.

4

Circularity and interconnection

Within systems, the process through which patterns of stability and change occur is a circular one rather than a linear one, therefore any action is a response to the other interactions within the system. By this process we can see that how one family member behaves is a direct response to the interactions of other family members, whether those interactions are directed towards that individual or merely observed by that individual. The behaviour of that one individual initiates further interactions in other family members. Any cause leads to an effect, which automatically becomes another cause. This is called *circularity*.

Let us take another example. A child is on his own in the kitchen and he stands on a chair to reach the ice cream in a fridge. He falls off the chair and breaks his leg. The mother who is at home has to take the child to the hospital and so she calls the father at work to come home to look after the other children. The father does this but is concerned about how this will affect his work schedule for the day. So after a few hours he rings up his mother to ask her if she will come over to look after the children and he returns to work. The grandmother, in looking after the other children, prepares them a meal but when the mother returns home she is concerned and upset as the wrong food has been used.

In the example above if we just think about what happened in terms of a limited straightforward linear cause and effect we might say that the events began with poor supervision by the mother. Then the father 'caused' his own mother to interfere with normal family routines (e.g. what got cooked). However, such a linear approach to cause and effect, which considers beginnings and endings, does not encapsulate the complexity of interactions in this simple example. A circular understanding on the other hand fails to find a beginning (a place to lay blame)

FAMILY THERAPY: 100 KEY POINTS

but rather understands the embedded nature of family life. On the contrary, by emphasising the contexts that affect family members, it encourages not blame but responsibility since all family members have a part to play in how things turn out.

Systems such as families are continually communicating and provide cycles of unbroken interaction between all parts and all levels of the system. As we have seen each and every family system communicates, receives communication and can be viewed as being its communication. This continuous endless looping of information exchange has no beginning and no end but is like a spiralling circle moving through time.

In such a conception of the family how does change occur? Such a question used to dominate family therapy thinking (Keeney 1983; Rivett and Street 2003). We have already noted that systems 'naturally' tend to reach a stable place but we have also noted that change is a constant feature of systems, especially given the movement of systems through time. Thus family therapists talk about the 'life cycle of families' (Carter and McGoldrick 1999), by which they mean that families have to manage developmental transitions constantly (see Point 9), but from a systemic point of view change occurs when new information *that does not fit the old established pattern of relationship* emerges. The family therapist therefore believes that the role of therapy is to introduce new information into the system. This new information might centre around the beliefs, feelings or behaviours of the family system (Carr 2000).

This new information must have a systemic consequence (e.g. the gestalt of the family system needs to be influenced by it). Because once it is accepted that the cycle of interaction is the unit of the system, this, rather than the individual, becomes the focus and primary source of change. The point is that individuals cannot be considered to be entirely free to act in new ways since they are, to some degree, defined and maintained by circular interactional patterns of which they are a part. From this perspective, it is affecting and attempting to alter the pattern of interactions through which changes are produced and these changes allow individuals to show different and new forms of behaviour. Family therapists frequently quote Bateson when they consider 'is this different enough?'. Bateson argued that systems change through 'news of difference' and that this difference needed to be 'the difference that makes a difference' (Bateson 1972: 453). This understanding of change suggests that family therapists are like 'therapeutic journalists', always looking for 'news' and 'hidden angles on a problem'. A less challenging metaphor would be to suggest that family therapists are like jazz musicians: looking for the space between notes and words in a task that seeks to help the family system improvise rather than play the standard tune.

5

Structures and contexts

As we have demonstrated, systems theory acknowledges that any definition of a system, of boundaries around systems, of structures and of meanings about systems are arbitrary, and that there must be systems within systems. The family is a subsystem of a community (and a culture and a political system) and within the family itself there will be component subsystems. The subsystems that are found within families describe the 'structure' of the family (Minuchin 1974). The family structure is just a way of considering how all the subsystems relate to each other to form different patterns of relationships within the family.

Each family member will be involved with other members differently. These different combinations are made of the inter-actions of particular sets of individuals, particularly in the way in which they occupy certain roles such as mother, father, part-ner, siblings, child–parent, grandparents and parents. Although the boundaries around the subsystems are arbitrary they do have a functional value because at particular times they pre-scribe a particular set of tasks for those individuals within that subsystem. For example, there clearly are a number of particular tasks of parenting that need to be performed by mature adults (the parents) rather than by say, other children. This subsystem has been termed the *executive subsystem* (Minuchin 1974). It could happen however that the executive subsystem, the parents, asks some older children to look after the younger children in some particular way that is appropriate for the ages of those concerned. As long as the parents remained in charge of this situation, and the older child does not become a permanent member of the executive subsystem, then a cooperative and flexible way of caring for the children and allowing them to develop skills as they grow up will occur.

Different families have different individuals operating within their varying subsystems. Within each family the circumstances delineated by subsystems and their interaction will result in the individuals behaving differently. The older brother looking after the younger sister is a different set of circumstances to the one where the two children are being cared for by their mother.

There are a considerable number of combinations of all the possible subsystems that are found within a family particularly if it has three generations in active involvement with each other. Typically the subsystems most frequently defined are the parenting subsystem, the child subsystem and a grandparenting subsystem. When the children and parents are in interaction this describes the child–parent subsystem. The 'structure' in this case will be how these delineated groups interrelate with each other in order to perform the tasks of living within the family. So although we are describing a structure made up of component parts, the boundaries between these particular parts will vary along the dimensions of fluidity, flexibility and functionality in their interaction in order to get the job of family living done.

Within the three-generational family we can see how one of the parents will be at the same time a child (of a grandparent), a parent (of a child), a sibling (of a brother/sister) and a partner (of a partner), so different individuals play different roles in different relational contexts. Clearly the way an adult child and an adult parent interact will be different from that of a young child and its parent. The person who is the grandparent is likely to behave very differently when they are dealing with their adult child alone compared to when they are dealing directly with the grandchild. Each set of subsystem interactions therefore creates different behaviours as the context is different in each case.

A context can therefore be defined as a recognisable pattern of events or ideas created by a family member that constructs a set of expectations about what is likely to happen. This helps people to plan their behaviour and it also provides meaning to those events. Contexts vary according to the expectation one has about how they should operate. For example a person who is a grandparent will expect to behave differently with their own child when they are discussing financial matters compared to when he/she is babysitting and looking after the infants in the family. Context is therefore not defined by the physical setting but by the expectation of how individuals should behave in that setting at that time. Families that are functioning adequately are able to recognise a greater number of contexts within their overall interaction and are able to adapt and change these contexts as the situation demands (Walsh 2003). Families who are less adaptable have less ability to vary their expectations and less ability to change contexts.

Pearce and Cronen (1980) suggest that even in each context it is helpful to see multiple systems at work. Thus in the decision to invite her husband to care for the children in the example in Point 4, the actual communication (e.g. 'please come home I have to take our son to hospital') was embedded in a context in which the mother knew she could ask for help from her husband. Some relationship contexts would not contain this assumption. For instance some relationships may assume that the first request for help would go to wider family (in this example the father's mother) or even the state. Equally, the relationship context is embedded within a history of that relationship and presumably a past experience of how this family copes with crisis. Thus we might assume that previous events have resulted in joint responsibility and the parents have 'mucked in' together. This relationship in turn is embedded in a context influenced by the experience of each partner in their original families (families of origin). Again the example might lead us to assume that joint decision making may have been common in these families and this may be a context that influences how this couple manage crises brought on by child accidents.

The advantage of thinking about interactional patterns being embedded in multiple contexts is that it allows the therapist to seek 'news of difference' at a number of different systemic levels, but it also points to the influence of the 'higher' contexts such as culture, state policy, institutional ideology and religious beliefs on how families manage day to day difficulties. Thus on the one hand diverse families such as gay and lesbian families or families from minority ethnic groups deal with similar everyday family contexts, but they also have to contend with cultures and institutional practices that may inhibit their usual ways of managing family problems. For instance, if in the example quoted in Point 4 the couple were a gay couple, getting away from work to care for the other children might have been seen as a family deficit within a work culture that discriminated against gay people. Thus the parent at work may be more fearful of losing his/her job if he left suddenly whereas a straight father would be seen as being a 'good caring dad' (McGoldrick and Hardy 2008).

6

Family rules, contexts and meanings

Each context within a family creates a set of expectations as to how one should behave within that context. Family members are very quick to perceive which particular context they are in at any particular time. Contexts can be created firstly by who is present, so, for example, if a mother and father are having a discussion about how to decorate the bathroom the children may recognise it as being an 'adult conversation' in which they have no invitation to contribute. They may then just ignore what goes on. The children here can be said to be following a family rule about not being involved in particular types of conversations that their parents may have.

Time and space also delineate some contexts. So, when a family is in the living room with the TV on and the six o'clock news is about to begin, family members will know that it is important that they are quiet so that Mum can listen to the news. In this situation it is assumed that the rule of how to behave is understood by everyone and so if somebody breaks that rule by chattering away it is likely that the person sitting next to them will be the one who tells them to be quiet. However, what may happen is that the 'chatterbox' continues. The emotional context subtly changes as family members expect Mum to get angry and they know that when she does it is safest to stay out of the limelight! Here is another important dimension that delineates a context: the emotional atmosphere. However, a 'Mother angry' together with 'Father angry' atmosphere will be a completely different context in which there will be different rules to follow not only by the children but also by the mother and father. Therefore contexts are all different depending on who is involved, the time, the place, the emotional atmosphere and the purpose of the interaction.

Often 'family rules' are best understood not in terms of what family members think are the rules but in how individuals typically behave in certain circumstances. For example in the 'Mother angry – Father angry' context what may occur is that the youngest child starts misbehaving, the oldest child tells the youngest child off, all the children start arguing, the mother leaves her argument with father and starts to deal with the children and father withdraws. Each element of this circular interactive chain can be said to be the 'rules' of that particular context.

A family therapist will always be alive to what constitutes these unspoken family rules. She will be seeking to describe them for the family and then see if alternative, different rules would work better for family members. Examples in clinical practice often revolve around how children become independent, what children are told and what is kept secret from them, who is to blame for family problems, which gender is responsible for which task and who says no and who says yes. Of particular importance will be the rules about the way in which the family relates to the outside world. Meeting professionals and talking about family difficulties to non-family members are contexts that are particularly rule bound and even though family members might struggle to articulate their family rules in these circumstances it is highly likely that all family members will behave in ways that follow 'rules'.

7

History and development

Although family processes are not linear, families themselves do exist in the linear dimension of time. As the family moves forward in time they have to deal with the predictable course of development as children are born, become adolescents, enter adulthood, create their own families, deal with ageing and then ultimately death (Carter and McGoldrick 1999). The stages of family life and development begin with the individual. Individual life cycles are the threads from which the overall family context is woven, with changes in the individual threads being reflected in the appearance and shape of a particular family life cycle. The most helpful way of considering how the family life cycle is organised is to focus on the notion of developmental task. These are issues that have to be dealt with so that the next set of issues on the path of development can be approached. Tasks by their very nature are relationship bound and involve interaction with other family members and by the generational effect, e.g. the tasks of one generation influence and are related to the tasks of another generation. Thus, for example, an individual requires some degree of personal auton-omy to meet the task of separating from parents and the parents need to be able to allow and even encourage this to happen. Hence the task of separating becomes a foundation for the task of forming relationships outside of the family and the task for the parents of allowing separation prepares for the couple tasks that follow after the child has left home. Clearly the 'solution' of any task is important for future development but what is of equal importance is the process of the solving itself. Indeed development both for the individual and the family is best conceived of as a continual process of facing tasks that being human sets. In this process, the cyclical nature of development is such that we can enter the process at any point and yet return to the same life cycle point within another generation.

Any position on the life cycle is, in itself, embedded in an evolving historical context that is ever changing, expanding or contracting.

All family members are potentially able to experience the role of every generation: A woman in her later years may have the experience of being a grandmother, a mother and a daughter. Even though we assume that these roles change over time, there is always a part of the self that is forever a daughter and forever a mother. Try as we may we are unable to lose the experience of childhood: the experience of being cared for in a certain way, of having certain behaviours expected of us and being given certain knowledge of ourselves and others. Naturally, if this is our experience, when we were children our parents were not only experiencing being parents but were also reliving aspects of their childhood while they cared for us. It is these issues that both link and separate the generations; these are issues that are truly trans-generational.

We can see therefore that within each family the process of history informs its members about ways of undertaking tasks. The family life cycle can be considered to be a process in which individuals learn how to be human and how to live within this particular family. The way in which we learn this will depend, to a considerable extent, on how our parents lived it and how their parents learnt it too.

Each person will be shown in their development certain ways of reacting to stress, being encouraged to relate to certain types of people and to have clear messages on how to produce and react to emotions. Each individual will be presented, through his or her family history, with a blueprint of how a male or female life should unfold. This 'script' will suggest or even demand that particular lifestyles are followed, that certain types of individuals are chosen as marital partners and that roles such as 'wayward child', 'clever person' and 'caring daughter' are followed. The script will provide the framework on which a person will construct a self image. To ensure that all scripts are interlocking within this developmental pattern, the family will have a series of 'myths' (Bagarozzi and Anderson 1989) in the form of stories or narratives of past family members. These stories tell people how roles are to be played out and what the major family rules are, and hence organise the family sense of identity.

This aspect of the family as a system has a number of clinical nuances to it. Family therapists talk about 'inter-generational' family scripts, which may or may not be helpful in helping families cope with adversity. Bowen (1972) and Lieberman (1980) developed ways of accessing these family scripts. Byng-Hall (1995) delineated two versions of family scripts: *replicative* and *corrective*. In the former, the old way of doing things passes down the generations; in the latter the new generation seeks to alter the script. More recent narrative therapists (White 2007) point out that because the family system is always changing, the past is also open to *reinterpretation* so nothing is certainly true about the past perception of family experience.

8

Meaning and time frames

The last few points can be summarised by understanding that families (human systems) are not only influenced by structures or feedback but also by meanings. Within families some inter-actional patterns happen in short time periods from seconds to hours, others go from days to weeks, others from weeks to years and yet others span at least one generation and beyond. With each family pattern there will be some agreement as to the 'meaning' of that pattern, i.e. how that particular interactive process is to be perceived, understood and then acted upon. Meaning is central to the interactional process. Within families there are different levels of meaning that also constitute a 'context' (Pearce and Cronen 1980). As in Points 5 and 6, we can begin with a speech act, which is a verbal or non-verbal message from one person to another. Then there is an episode, which is a short pattern of reciprocated interaction. At the next level is a relationship, which is the conception of how and on what terms two or more people engage in interaction over longer periods of time. The next level of meaning is a life script, which involves a person's conception of their self in interaction throughout their development, and finally we have the family myth (Bagarozzi and Anderson 1989), which includes general conceptions of how personal roles and family relationships work and how that family relates to the outside world.

There is a process of influence between these levels of mean-ing, with family myths informing individual scripts, which in turn inform how relationships work, etc. But it is also the case that the episodes, interaction and life scripts might be influenced by the context 'below' them. Let us take an example. A family might struggle when coping with an anorexic child and feel that they can do nothing to help and rely on 'outside' agencies to solve their problem. Careful discussion might unlock a family myth, which came down from the previous generation, that mental illness was uncontrollable and beyond the resources of the family to manage. If this families' individual episodes of success in fighting the anorexia are then punctuated, the family myth might be exposed to be just that: a myth with no more power over the present situation than a toothless monster.

Families use meaning in order to deal with the amount of information that bombards them in their social relationships. The meanings that are constructed are ways of categorising information and then linking these categories together so that in some way they organise and then help to predict how the world will work. Individuals can agree about who disagrees about the meaning of any particular event and their perceptions of how other people understand an event may be accurate or inaccurate. When individuals share meanings they can act in unison; when they have different sets of meaning but can perceive how the others see the situation then there is a foundation for negotiation of joint action. If individuals are inaccurate in their perception of how the other person constructs meaning then it is likely that there will be conflict. Similarly conflict arises when even though people have a similar view of meaning they wrongly think that they have different views.

Within any family therefore each member will be constructing his/her own set of meanings for any behavioural event. This set of meanings will then dictate how the past is viewed, how the present is dealt with and how the future is planned. Some meanings will be shared and others will only be held by individuals. It is this matrix of meaning that will constitute what can be termed the 'family ideology' (Palazzoli *et al.* 1978; Dallos 1991). The stronger the degree of agreement, the more cohesive the family ideology will be, though it has to be remembered that there can be a family ideology 'that we always disagree'. The way in which a family operates together and their shared meanings are associated with that family's sense of its special identity as a group. This involves the values the family members hold, the beliefs and ideas they share and the family ideology expressed or otherwise that they espoused about how they operate in the world. The shared meanings within any family are important because they relate to membership of the family; shared meaning indicates who is included and who is not a part of the family.

These ideas about meanings inform a number of family therapy practices. Firstly, they explain why family therapists will carefully uncover what matters to each family they work with. They will explore what 'kind' of a family the family see themselves as and they will help parents explain what they expected/ wanted when they first made the transition from a couple to a family. Secondly, it explains why family therapists are keen not only to discover difference in contexts, patterns and feelings between family members but also difference in meanings. For instance, a child might interpret a parent's anger as 'meaning' that he or she is unloved, but other family members may interpret the same anger as evidence that the parent is overburdened. This respectful elaboration of meanings can provide the 'difference that makes the difference'.

9

The life cycle and transitions

In order to appreciate the developmental flow of family life and the tasks that are associated with this, it is important to consider the way the family moves from one phase of life to another and therefore the idea of a transition becomes important. A transition refers to the process of change or instability that occurs when the family system moves from one relatively stable pattern to another relatively stable pattern (Carter and McGoldrick 1989). We can see that the overall developmental process is a dynamic one of oscillation between stability and change. Transitions do not include the continuous minor adjustments in the behaviour of the family and its members but refer to periods of time when the family becomes used to and adapts to a new set of circumstances. Usually the circumstances are described as being 'normative' in that they are frequently occurring events in any particular culture that many, if not most, families will encounter throughout their life. This applies to the variety and diversity of families that we have already described: nuclear families, stepfamilies, lone parent families and extended families.

For example when a couple has their first child a great many changes happen. The pattern of dependency changes, with the needs of the child having to take a priority over the immediate needs of the adults. One adult may remain at home to look after the child and this will have an effect on how the family deal with their time spent together. Household tasks will expand and need to be redistributed. Financial conditions will change with the reliance on one primary wage earner, which itself will subtly alter the way the couple negotiate expectations of each other. The transition extends outwards from this immediate family subsystem as it may be that both parents decided they will return to work and they seek the involvement of the grandparents to child-mind the infant during the working day. Although the grandparents may be willing to do this it will have an effect on how they live their lives and on how they relate to their children who are now parents.

The most obvious transitions within a family in our western culture involve the setting up of a home together, the birth of a new child, children beginning school and then leaving home, retirement and the death of a partner. However, there are other reasonably normative transitions (Walsh 2003). Such is the frequency of divorce in our culture that the process of relationships breaking up and children having to form new patterns of interrelating with a parent living elsewhere can also be considered to be normative.

There will be however, in each family's development, some unique transitional events that have a meaning and significance solely to the people involved. An example of this would be one of the adults in the family obtaining an unpredicted but significant promotion. This might affect where the family needs to live, how available that adult is for family tasks and how the financial situation of the family stands.

10

Transitions and stress

As the family moves forward in time it has to deal with pressures that come from the predictable course of development. In family life cycle terminology, the time dimension of development is called a horizontal process (Carter and McGoldrick 1989). These provide their own stressors, ones that arise from the history of the family, which include patterns of relating and functioning that are transmitted down the generations (transgenerational stresses). These stressors include all the family attitudes, taboos, expectations, labels and loaded issues with which each member grows up.

But the unique events discussed above are classed as vertical processes, which are often more challenging than the above example. Examples of such unpredictable processes are chronic illness, untimely death, accident, divorce and remarriage. Systems theory would suggest that the family system has its own ways of adjusting to major transitions but the pressure to adjust to multiple transitions (horizontal and vertical) may be overwhelming. Thus the birth of a child is a challenge to most couples. If that child had a major disability and the parents were made redundant as a result of missing work to care for the child, then the family resources would be seriously impaired. With such a situation, the family therapist would be helping the family to rebuild its resources and widen the context of family support.

Stress in the family's development is at its highest level as the family moves from one phase of life to another. Where felt anxiety, doubt and uncertainty are experienced, then one can consider there being a transitional crisis. This transitional stress is one in which new meanings and new structures are needed in order to successfully adapt to the change. In themselves transitions are not necessarily stressful, but some transitions become particularly problematic because other external stressors impinge on the families' coping mechanism. Many of the unpredictable events of life also demand changes that require a transition to a different means of functioning, for example the birth of a handicapped child or the onset of a chronic illness will involve considerable family changes. Some families, because of their history, deal with particular transitions very well but not so well with others. However, it is important that in emphasising how families deal with stress we not only consider the need for flexibility and adaptability in the face of transitional demands but also consider the family's ability to maintain stability. It is important to concentrate on *managing change* as well as recognising the value of maintaining things as they are.

Therefore not only do we need to consider the internal processes of how a family operates but how those internal processes manage the external system that impinges upon it. Some families will have difficulties with particular 'normal' transitions, whereas others will find difficulty in dealing with unexpected transitions. Each family in its own way will encounter problems at some time and each in its own way will need to find its way of dealing with a transition and dealing with the stress of that transition. Hence, although 'normative' change in any culture is stressful to varying degrees, when developmental stresses intersect with trans-generational or vertical stress there is a considerable increase of anxiety in the system, which may result in the family system 'breaking down'.

This part has outlined the major aspects of systems theory. Systems theory is like the bequeathed gift for generations of family therapists. Like many such bequests, sometimes it is forgotten, occasionally it is repudiated but usually it is simply 'there' beneath the everyday practice of family therapy. What systems theory invites is a focus on relationship, pattern and context. It provides a way of thinking about family life and the problems that arise in the process of living together as intimately connected individuals. It transcends the particular 'form' of the family by emphasising process. Systems theory has also provided some major ideas about how to help families. The overriding principle is one of respect for this 'natural system' and its members. However, systems theory posits that change occurs by changes in relationship either through changes in behaviour, meanings or feelings about those relationships. Lastly, it is difference that, brought to the attention of the family, leads to change.

Part 2

COMPLEXITIES AND MISUNDERSTANDINGS

11

Doesn't systems theory make it sound as if people are 'things'?

It is important to remember that systems theory, which has become central to family therapy practice, originated in areas of study that did not include human interaction. Thus the early ideas from systems theory were founded on the study of mechanical systems (Becvar and Becvar 1999). Later these aspects of systems theory were applied to robotics and cybernetic systems (including inter-continental ballistic missiles). From a historical viewpoint, systems theory entered therapeutic practice largely through the influence of Gregory Bateson (1972, 1979). Although Bateson was an anthropologist, his family background had made him aware of the 'biological system' (his father was a biologist) and in the post war years he saw systems theory as a theory that could unify a number of areas of human knowledge. After his studies with family therapists, Bateson went on to apply systems theory to other animal 'systems', including otters. It is therefore not surprising that some therapists, including some family therapists, feel uncomfortable with applying a concept that originated within the physical sciences to the realm of human relationships. After all, human beings are not machines and as such their responses are not as predictable as systems theory might imply. Indeed, perhaps what makes human beings *not* mechanical is their ability to create meaning. Therefore, some commentators have sought to revise systems theory and rather than seeing it as a mechanical metaphor for family life have seen it as a meaning-making structure. Bogdan (1984) for instance saw the family system as an 'ecology of ideas' and Anderson and Goolishian (1988) stated that 'human systems are linguistic systems' (1988: 373). These authors argued that systems theory with its ideas about feedback loops, recurring patterns and boundaries could not explain how families and individuals changed or how each individual *felt* within their network of relationships.

These objections and others have fuelled a growth in alternatives to systems theory for family therapy practice (White and Epston 1990). Indeed, family therapy text books can be divided between those that expound systems theory (like this one) and those that don't (Lowe 2004). In this book, we propose that systems theory, even though it has significant problems as a coherent and complete theory of human interaction, provides significant benefits to the practitioner working with families. These benefits are that systems theory highlights *relationship, interaction, pattern and collective change.* This contrasts with the emphasis of many other therapies, which highlight *internal experience, past traumas and individual action for change.*

When it comes to 'literal' understandings of systems theory, it has another gift to offer. Because systems theory assumes that in human relationships there will be different perspectives, it inevitably assumes that no one perspective is 'true'. In the language of family therapy, we hold all perspectives 'with a light touch'. This attitude will be described later as curiosity (Point 27) but it also presumes a respect or commitment to uncertainty. Clearly, this also reflexively applies to systems theory itself. Thus, even systems theory should be seen as a metaphor rather than a truth: Within family therapy, systems theory is a map, not what is actually *out there*. Bateson (1972) himself was fond of quoting an old Zen story, which states that the moon's reflection in the water is not the moon; the finger that points to the moon is not the moon; *the map is not the territory.* In this sense, systems theory is not literally true when it is applied to family life, it is merely a metaphorical explanation. Pocock (1995) has maintained, like many others, that the metaphor of systems as applied to families is only useful as far as it is useful! Equally, Roffman (2005) and Simon (1992) argue that family therapists in contemporary practice need to support a 'soft' version of systems theory.

12

Doesn't family therapy ignore the individual?

One of the consequences of attending to interactions and patterns in relationships is that family therapists may be seen as ignoring individual experiences and even regarding the family as more important than the individual family member. This has been another common criticism of systems theory (Rivett and Street 2003). Some authors have called this the *reification* (making the family a 'solid' 'real' entity) of the family. Traditionally, such critiques have come from commentators who have been alive to the domination of individuals by family processes and have wanted family therapists to promote social justice or a more contextual understanding of family life (Poster 1978). The common systems axiom that 'the whole is more than the sum of its parts' can be regarded as legitimising this perspective, e.g. the parts are less important than the whole. Some authors have argued that family therapy came into existence at precisely the moment when social conditions required a happy compliant work force in which family life ensured this compliance (Rose 1999). From this view, systems theory legitimated a form of therapy that privileged family functioning *against* individual (rebellious) development.

It is certainly true that early family therapy writing rarely addressed issues of social justice and individual experience. It is also true that 'shorthand' phrases like 'schizogenic' or 'anorectic' family seem to imply that the family as a whole has a defining role over individuals. And yet, if this perspective is taken in the 'light' way suggested in Point 11, it is hard to deny that on one level human relationships do constrain what is possible for an individual. If we exclude those contextual limitations such as material resources, we notice that it is 'what others expect of us' that limits what we do. This has been described in the aphorism: 'It is the ones we love who keep us the way we are'. Most of us spend our lives balancing investment in relationships with investment in ourselves.

There is a further hidden criticism about systems theory embedded within the one above. This is the idea that family therapists rarely explore individual experience and fail to encourage the expression of emotions. If we imagine for a moment that a psychodynamic therapist is observing a family therapy session. This therapist would see the family therapist exploring relationship patterns and asking how one family member's feelings had been understood by another rather than asking the question 'how does that make you feel?'. The psychodynamic therapist might then comment that no 'in depth' emotional work has been done. It is certainly true that family therapists, because of systems theory, concentrate upon relationships rather than the process of emotional catharsis (unburdening of feelings).

However, it is clear that the 'stuff' of therapy is how individual family members experience each other as thinking, acting and feeling people and the competent family therapist would explore individual experience if this was clinically and humanly important. There is ample evidence that family therapists work with situations where individuals have experienced trauma and abuse (Woodcock 2001) in which healing requires the compassionate discovery of the 'unsaid' traumatic experience. But once more the emphasis within family therapy is to enable the family group to help in the healing and not prevent healing by unhelpful patterns or responses. In other words, the focus remains upon the system but does not disregard the individual.

13

What about the 'self' of the therapist?

The idea that family therapists have viewed the 'family' as a reified concept has also fuelled another criticism of this form of therapy. Many who have previously been trained in one of the individual focused therapies have argued that family therapists lack an understanding of the role of the therapeutic *self* within the therapeutic context (Baldwin 2000). The argument is that the 'family' is seen as an objective set of relationships that an objective 'outsider' can influence via therapy with no reference to the internal workings of that outsider.

Interestingly, this criticism does have some relevance in the history of family therapy. For instance, Haley (1981), one of the most provocative of the early family therapists, argued that therapy for the therapist was not required as this only led to failed forms of therapy (he was a critic of psychodynamic therapy). However, in the 1980s, systems theory was revised to include what became known as 'second order cybernetics' (Becvar and Becvar 1999). This version of systems theory asserts that what is seen is influenced by the prejudices and limitations of the seer. Becvar and Becvar (1999) for instance state that 'as we observe, we influence that which we are attempting to understand . . . we do not discover behaviour, we create it' (1999: 36). This new way of understanding systems theory radically altered how family therapists understood their practice. It also brought in an awareness of how the therapeutic team was influenced by their own biases. These biases became recognised as being built on family of origin experience, class, gender, sexual orientation, race and culture. In family therapy terms, this evolution led to the growth of a form of therapy called 'second order family therapy', which was promulgated by Lynn Hoffman (Hoffman 1993, 2002) who herself had a long history of working with the early family therapy pioneers. This 'second order' family therapy integrated the therapeutic self into the therapy, encouraged collaborative practice and established changes in the way family therapists used teams.

Like any 'new' version of a therapy, proponents of second order family therapy approaches tended to forget previous practices that contradicted their view of history. Thus there were examples of family therapists regarding the self of the therapist as important even in earlier forms of family therapy (Kaslow 1987; Lieberman 1987; Street 1989). However, the arrival of second order cybernetics did make more acceptable the growing emphasis on self development for family therapists in training and autonomous practice (Hildebrand 1998) and we outline this emphasis in Points 73–80.

14

Doesn't family therapy ignore the social contexts of families?

Many of the critics who asserted that family therapy reified the family also argued that family therapy took the family out of its social context. This view has a number of aspects and has been developed by a number of very prominent family therapists themselves. Poster (1978) for instance, writing from a left wing perspective, believed that family therapists ignored the power of social contexts and assumed that the only system worth investigating was the family system. On the contrary he argued that class relations, poverty and structural inequality were more likely to be determinants of family problems than family dynamics. He argued that since structural factors were likely to cause any 'dysfunctional' relationships, therapy was clearly going to fail.

These views have been levelled at all forms of therapy (Pilgrim 1992, 1997) and have been echoed by family therapists, who have argued that the field should attend to inequality within their consulting rooms (Carpenter 1987; Epstein 1993). Implicit in the assumption that family therapy ignores certain contextual factors is the idea that family therapy sees the 'cause' of problems as residing in family dynamics (Morton 1987). This latter view has most recently been criticised by Eisler (2005), who comments that the dynamics that family therapists see in families with problems are as likely to be the result of adapting to the problems as causative of those problems.

In a sense, this criticism fails to understand that systems theory allows for multiple levels of understanding for family problems. Indeed, some family therapists accept that there are multiple levels of context (Pearce 1994) that influence any particular difficulty and that the therapy could usefully be centred upon the most relevant context at any particular time. For instance, therapy may revolve around helping a family to consider how they can improve their social context as much as it can revolve around parental conflict. Indeed, forms of contemporary narrative family therapy would do just this (White 2007). The crucial issue here is 'what is the most likely level at which intervention will help the family cope better?'. Family therapists therefore may respond to a family's difficulties by working with schools, with peer groups and with community groups if the therapist thinks that this is important and can be encompassed within their professional role. Recent interventions for difficult teenagers for instance are often called *multi-systemic therapy* (Sheidow *et al.* 2003) and work on all these levels. It is also true that some family therapists have concentrated on working with 'the families of the poor' (Minuchin *et al.* 1998) with the explicit aim of empowering them in the face of their social exclusion.

However, family therapy, like all therapies, focuses upon how those in therapy can take responsibility for making their lives better. As such its language is about how to empower families within the format of therapy: Therapy has political aspects to it, but it is not a political context per se. Goldner (1991) has put this distinction most eloquently when talking about gender:

> Once it becomes absolutely clear that psychotherapy is nothing more and nothing less than talk, then it is best to conceive of family therapy as a rhetorical strategy that helps elucidate the dilemmas of love and power between men and women living in a patriarchal society.
>
> (1991: 59)

The same view holds for all the other contextual pressures that families experience: Family therapy elucidates the constraints in order to help families grasp whatever change is possible within and beyond those contexts.

15

Is family therapy sexist?

There have been other powerful objections to the way systems theory and, by implication, family therapy ignore social context. These have come from feminist practitioners and practitioners who recognised that a limited understanding of systems theory prevented family therapists from working creatively with diverse and sometimes socially excluded groups. The feminist critique asserted that by concentrating upon 'family', family therapists ignored the social construction of gender (McGoldrick *et al.* 1991). This meant that early family therapy models assumed that the gender roles evident within the 'traditional nuclear family' were appropriate and enduring, whilst from a feminist point of view such roles were often constraining for women (and girls) and were part of a socially imposed patriarchy.

This critique was particularly pertinent where therapists worked with issues of abuse. In such situations, it was argued that if a family therapist held to a rigid version of systems theory, he would assume that all family members had equal access to power and influence (Dell 1989). This clearly did not hold true, either in most families or in cases of domestic violence or child sexual abuse. Accordingly, the argument went, victims would be blamed for 'causing' their abuse and perpetrators would escape responsibility (Kaufman 1992).

It should be clear that only a very narrow understanding of systems theory would lead to such assumptions. Moreover, systems theory is perfectly able to allow for the levels of complexity implicit in these arguments. One of the key questions that family therapists will be asking themselves when they meet a new family system is 'who holds what kind of power?'. As a metaphor for understanding human relationships, systems theory suggests that each individual affects others and some part of their concept of self is relational. It does not assert that each person influences each other equally. Moreover, from an ethical perspective, family therapy practice must conform to seeking an end to abusive relationships and family therapists must intervene to protect vulnerable family members. Indeed, many of the feminist family therapy writers have made immense contributions to family therapy practice. Now a competent family therapist would be required to be gender sensitive and to explore with families how their interpretations of gender roles may constrain and prevent the expression of their full potential in relation to each other (Rivett and Street 2003).

It might also be suggested that family therapy, with its understanding about levels of context, its use of circular questions and its stance of curiosity, is ideally placed to explore gender inequalities within therapy. In most families there are meanings attached to money, food and maybe regular patterns of behaviour such as cooking, cleaning (including toilets) and caring. All of these if explored with circular questions will reveal gender assumptions and may be connected to the problem that has brought a family to therapy. It therefore might be argued that, of all the therapies, family therapy with its use of systems theory is most able to do what Goldner has suggested: to 'elucidate the dilemmas of love and power between men and women living in a patriarchal society' (Goldner 1991: 59).

16

Does family therapy promote what it sees as a 'normal family'?

The previous point demonstrated that early versions of family therapy may have been influenced by the context within which they emerged. This has continued to be an issue for family therapy. If we consider as an example the model of family transitions and the family life cycle that we discussed earlier, it would be easy to read this model as suggesting that 'normal' families go through these stages. Therefore, it might imply that a family that does not do so is somehow 'abnormal' and as such may be seen therapeutically as in need of 'revision'. When we recognise that very few families in the western world conform to this model, and we notice the different types of family around the world, we see how absurd such a notion is.

Even in the western world, families are vividly diverse (Muncie *et al.* 1997). Nock (2000) has pointed out how marriage, cohabitation, fertility, child rearing and family patterning have all undergone major changes in the last 50 years (Robinson 1997; Gorell Barnes 1998). Migration and immigration have also brought varied family structures to these societies. The recognition that respect and human rights should permeate society have ensured that gay and lesbian families are thriving whilst reproductive techniques mean that children are born into families with many different forms.

In this context, if family therapy asserted that there is a template for the 'best' or 'normal' family it would be betraying its curious, open stance and it would be ignoring the vast number of families that it is meant to help. In fact, again, such a criticism of systems theory is overly simplistic. It may be more helpful to think not in terms of 'norms' but in terms of 'tasks'. Thus all families in which children are living need to manage the task of nurturing those children into adulthood. This will apply to lesbian families, South Asian families, communes as well as heterosexual 'two parent' families. On this level systems theory and the family life cycle theory are *process* theories, not normative theories. On the contrary, systems theory leads us to ask of any particular family system 'what aspects of relationship are not helping the family members reach their potential?' rather than assuming that there are blanket rules for what works best. From this way of thinking very few psychotherapies are as well placed to work with diverse family groups as family therapy, for its theory places difference and multi-perspectives onto the centre of the therapeutic stage.

This view is shown in the rich variety of clinical literature that explores such work within the family therapy world (McGoldrick *et al.* 1996; McGoldrick and Hardy 2008). It is also the case that the central approach of family therapists, which is that of curiosity and uncertainty, facilitates an openness to diversity that permeates family therapy.

17

Is there such a thing as one 'family therapy'?

To an outsider, the number of 'kinds' of family therapy can be bewildering. The literature is full of terms such as 'structural family therapy', 'Milan family therapy', 'systemic family therapy' and 'narrative family therapy', to name only a few. Here we wish to briefly outline the major developments in the history of family therapy, highlighting the major 'schools'. We also want to summarise what *unites* these schools and emphasise what is common to them all.

There are many histories of family therapy (Nichols and Schwartz 1998; Dallos and Draper 2005) and inevitably all of them emphasise different aspects of that history (Rivett and Street 2003). According to one version, family therapy emerged during the 1960s and 1970s as systems theory was applied to family life. During this phase a number of schools of family therapy developed, most notably structural family therapy, which was created by Minuchin (1974), and strategic family therapy, created by Haley (1976). The defining styles of these forms of family therapy were that the therapist was an active agent of change and set tasks for families that were designed to alter their habitual ways of managing problems. It was the emergence of the Milan school of family therapy during the 1970s and early 1980s that shifted the field into working with family meanings and also with working with some of the most difficult presentations such as psychosis and anorexia.

The Milan school (Palazzoli *et al.* 1978) instituted the use of teams as an integral part of family therapy and developed the use of circular questions as an intervention in itself. These two phases of development have been called 'first order' because they assumed that the family could be influenced and changed by the intervention of the therapist. In other words they relied on 'first order cybernetics/systems theory'. During the 1980s and 1990s this 'first order' view changed and 'second order' cybernetics encouraged family therapists to consider their own role in the therapy. Hoffman (1993) is the most significant developer of this concept and she was influenced herself by ideas about reflexive practice and feminism. During these years the feminist critique challenged the 'smug' ideas that therapists 'knew best' (Walters 1990; McGoldrick *et al.* 1991). At the same time family therapists reviewed their practice with diverse families, including those from minority ethnic populations and from gay and lesbian families. Equally, they concluded that they had failed to include in their practice the role of institutional oppression and the biases of the therapist him or herself. In this phase of family therapy, Andersen introduced the idea of the team reflecting in front of the family (Andersen 1991) and a collaborative approach to therapy became established (Anderson and Gehart 2007).

It was also during this time that ideas from postmodernism entered the field; in particular a narrative approach to practice emerged (White and Epston 1990). Some family therapy historians would class this postmodernist form of family therapy as a 'third wave' in the development of family therapy. Others (Dallos and Urry 1999) would argue that during the late 1990s a 'third order' family therapy emerged that integrated the lessons from the previous decades. Thus Dallos and Urry (1999) believe that contemporary family therapy attends to structures and meanings whilst involving the whole self of the therapist in the therapy.

This complex history of family therapy might suggest that 'family therapy' as a field has no unity. Some say that there is no such thing as family therapy, only a collection of 'family therapies' (Reimers and Street 1993). It would be erroneous to assume that such variety is a product of the past: Modern texts attest to the fact that there continue to be a multitude of forms of family therapy (Lebow 2005). We must also note that some therapies that started as family therapies are now almost devoid of an interactional component such as narrative therapy and brief solution-focused therapy. On the other hand, the practice of family therapy is now increasingly one in which ideas and techniques of all the different stages of family therapy development are used by practitioners within a unified whole. There is less and less reliance on 'one' school of family therapy (Rivett 2008). Indeed, Lebow (2005) argues that family therapy has never been so unified because the value of seeing individuals in context and problems within interactional cycles has continued to gather evidence of success.

There is therefore a legacy of systems theory for family therapy. This legacy determines that family therapy notices relational patterns, it understands behaviour within a matrix of beliefs and generational experiences, it understands that the individual is radically connected to others and it privileges working with multi-generational groupings. Systems theory also gives a certain therapeutic stance to the family therapist. Being a witness to the family system encourages a curiosity, a valuing of difference and an awareness of self within multiple systems, all of which constitute the family therapy task.

Part 3

BEGINNING THERAPY

18

Collaborative integrative ethical therapy model

An important starting point for developing the skills and practice of family therapy is the appreciation of its collaborative, integrative and ethical basis. Contemporary practice integrates many of the original family therapy skills with techniques that have evolved in the almost 50-year history of family therapy (Pinsof 1995; Sexton *et al.* 2003; Rivett 2008). This integration represents a unified core of family therapy practice.

However, one of the overriding principles of this integration is that of collaboration. In Point 16 we highlighted that early family therapists believed that they could help families without collaborating with them (at least in the way we mean the term now). In the 2000s this is neither possible nor ethical. It might be argued that a collaborative approach to the family therapy represents the success of new wave collaborative family therapies, or perhaps it is the recognition that professional practice needs to be accountable in the modern era. Collaborative here means that the therapist respects the views of family members, and seeks to work with them in an open genuine relationship. In this sense, family therapy must be ethical as well: respecting the diversity of families, never asking family members to discuss what they don't want to discuss and taking responsibility for the safety of family members. It is equally important that the therapist respects the wider systemic 'causes' for family problems. Ethical family therapy practice will always attend to the wider systems that have an impact upon family life and the difficulties that families have. For instance, in a situation where a family are asked to come for therapy because a school has concerns about their daughter, the family therapist would want to help the family think about how the culture of the school might be influencing their child as well as whether the family itself has a view about the school. It is not uncommon for families in such situations to blame the school for their child's problems. In the therapy room, the therapist would want to track family attitudes to school and how the parents envisage their child in the future with or without a 'solid' educational experience. This conversation might again spread out over generations and link behaviours to attitudes.

This is only one example. Many family therapists would use their curiosity to help families understand how they are themselves 'dominated' by social and cultural expectations. When working with a young person who is anorexic, this might mean helping her explore the meanings of female 'thinness' in our society (size 'zero' discussions). Such a conversation may (but not necessarily) be part of an externalising conversation (see Point 65) that helps the young person see how the 'self' they have accepted is one that may not be the one they prefer.

An equally ethical concern is for family therapy practice to be cognisant of the current evidence base and reflect this as much as is possible. Such a reflection does not need to mean that family therapy needs to replicate research manuals, for instance where a family member is depressed (Sexton *et al.* 2008), but it does mean that because research suggests that couple dynamics and loss are significant factors in depression (Jones and Asen 2000), these are themes that need to be explored in the therapy. Most of the evidence base for family therapy confirms that the interactive focus of the modality contributes significantly to the improvement of symptoms, but there may be additional focuses that will improve outcomes even further. Thus most family therapists will also incorporate psycho-educational aspects to their work (Point 67) for instance.

19

Who is the customer?

In their everyday life families come into contact with a variety of professional people such as doctors, teachers, nurses, solicitors, physiotherapists, social workers, etc. who provide them with a variety of personal services. When the family experiences some difficulty with one of its members and help is provided, people outside of the family become involved and a new system is created, which we can term the *problem-determined system* (Anderson and Goolishian 1988). These other individuals collaborate with the family system to aid with the issue with which the family are confronted. On some occasions family members will seek out help from such individuals themselves. For example, a mother may go to her general practitioner when she is concerned about the behaviour of her eight-year-old son. On other occasions using a similar example some professionals such as the school headmaster may request to see the parents because of the boy's difficult behaviour in the classroom. Some problem-determined systems are therefore created voluntarily by the family and others are created by outsiders who want the family to 'do something'. In both of these examples the doctor or the headmaster may suggest to the parents that they accept a referral to an agency that provides family therapy. A new system will then come into being, which will be composed of the therapist and those who attend for the therapy session – this is the *therapy system.*

In some therapy situations, the client arrives with the clear request 'I have a problem. I think therapy may help me with it.' This unfortunately is not often the case in family therapy. Typically family members, and usually not all family members, present themselves as individuals who are concerned about one of their number. They believe this person has a particular diffi-culty that they, the family members, hope would benefit from some outside help. Their own contribution may be minimised or they may personally feel themselves to be the cause of the difficulty or they may see the problem as being one that is essentially outside of their own family (see Point 3). In our example, the mother may come along to see the therapist as she is concerned that her son is developing bad behaviour, whereas if the school asked the parents to get help they may think that the headmaster has more of a problem with their son than they do. Families and other 'caring agencies' do not automatically have a systemic understanding of family life and may identify different family members as being the 'problem'.

All families therefore arrive for therapy with some preconceived notions and set expectations about what the problem is about and how it may be tackled. Indeed, the referring professional will similarly have preconceived notions in the same way that may or may not agree with how particular family members see the problem (Palazzoli *et al*. 1980b; Street and Downey 1996). Whenever there is a difficulty with a person and it does not seem to go away, the most natural reaction from everyone is that it must be somebody's fault: 'If only he, the boy, listened to me more we wouldn't have this trouble' or 'If only he, the headmaster, admitted he had inexperienced teachers we wouldn't have this problem'.

The natural process in a referral for family therapy therefore is one in which, from the outset, the therapist has to be mindful of the process by which blame and responsibility for difficulties are described by the problem-determined system. If there is an agreement on perspectives it is likely that one person is seen as being the cause of the difficulty rather than the problem having an interactive base. These perspectives have to be acknowledged and explored from the outset of therapy. It is the system that presents itself as the customer and not the individual. The family therapist attends immediately to these differing perspectives and uses language carefully to avoid any assumption that any one description is the 'right' one. Equally, the family therapist avoids 'blaming' statements by always describing the interactional components of the problem presented rather than accepting that one person is responsible for the problem. An example would be not that 'Robert is naughty' but 'Robert's Mum finds his behaviour difficult to manage'.

20

Contacting and convening

There are a variety of routes by which a family arrives in the family therapy situation:

1   One professional may make a referral to another professional with a clear specification that family therapy is required.
2   A professional to professional referral may occur, specifying the problem, and after an assessment it is considered that family therapy should be offered to deal with the difficulty.
3   The professional himself may have met with a part of the family system as part of some other professional task, a task that on assessment appears best dealt with within a family therapy framework. In these circumstances the professional becomes a family therapist for a definite period of time in order to meet particular goals that are defined within the general professional role.

Whatever the route in order to initiate the therapeutic process the therapist will need to communicate to those most obviously involved so that a meeting can be arranged. It is the therapist's job to convene the therapy system. Certainly there are a number of means by which professionals can now contact people (via email and text) but it is important from the outset that the therapist is mindful of the communication process between himself and family members. The most usual practice is to write a letter to all the family clearly stating that it is helpful to meet all family members on the first visit and therefore if everybody could attend it would prove beneficial:

> Example: Dear Mr and Mrs Jones and Robert,
> Your family doctor, Dr Taylor, has asked me to meet with you to discuss the problems that you are having in the

family. I would be pleased to see you all at two o'clock on the 24th of June in my office. Please let me know if this is convenient.

In many senses this is a very straightforward appointment letter except that it needs to be personally sent by the professional and not just come from an agency with someone else signing it. Families are more likely to attend if they know the name of the person they are meeting rather than encounter some aspect of a bureaucratic system (Street 1994). A letter is also a much more public form of communication that different individuals, especially those to whom the letter is addressed, are free to look at and come to their own view. It is a form of communication that is the least likely to involve one family member translating its meaning to another and therefore it is the most direct communication to all family members. Sometimes, the therapist will know that only one family member will be able to read the English in the letter. In this case the letter should be translated into whatever language is appropriate.

This letter contains all the necessary information, both direct and indirect. Directly it provides a place, time and way to contact the professional concerned. Indirectly it is addressed firstly to the adults and by placing the parents first it structurally and politely acknowledges the centrality of this couple to the family. Next it also indicates that Robert requires an invitation in his own right. The letter identifies the person who made the referral and the nature of his request that the family members be seen. The problem is then mentioned by reference to a general difficulty identified by the referral. The letter also carries with it the invitation for 'all' to attend and obviously the family will interpret this in their own way. In this case the mother may attend with the child herself; the parents may come on their own; the parents and the grandmother may attend with a child or the parents may send the grandmother and the child on their own. Whatever scenario appears, it should be appreciated that whoever attends is the family's response to that situation. It is a form of communication that 'means' something. It is their solution to the attendance problem and they will have obviously taken the action that makes the most sense to them. It would be the family's first statement of their perspective or, to put it more accurately, the dominant perspective on this issue and as such it needs to be acknowledged. The therapist should therefore be ready to acknowledge this decision and accept it. For example, if only child and mother come, the therapist might ask how the family decided that Mr Jones did not need to come and would enquire if this means something about how family problems are managed (Haley 1976).

21

Meeting the individuals

At the initial meeting there are several clear tasks. The therapist needs to say 'hello' to everyone and then to introduce both herself and the general professional task. She needs to set her understanding of the context of the meeting by being clear to the family about what is known. The family need to be able to offer their description of the problem and from this the therapist will be able to clarify the family's expectation of the meeting.

It is usual for everybody to be somewhat anxious before they meet a professional to discuss personal issues. This anxiety is because people don't know what will happen and what they 'have to do'. Therapists can easily forget how stressful this process can be (Reimers and Treacher 1995). It is therefore important from the outset that the therapist implies a gentle control of the situation that puts people at ease but also in a way that softly directs how the communication within this new system will work. The best place to begin this is with the greeting of everybody and the settling of people down into the session.

Therapist:	Hello I am Joan Watson and I work here as a therapist. Are you Mrs Jones?
Mrs Jones:	Yes that's right.
Therapist:	I'm very pleased to meet you. Please take a seat.
Mrs Jones:	Anywhere?
Therapist:	Yes that's fine. I guess you must be Mr Jones?
Mr Jones:	Yes. Pleased to meet you.
Therapist:	And this must mean that you are Robert? I'm very pleased to meet you. (*The therapist ensures that he has direct eye contact with the boy.*) I would say to you that you can sit where you like but your mum and dad have

only left that seat between them for you. Is
that going to be comfortable for you?

A straightforward beginning, but for the family therapist it is important to be mindful about all elements of interaction and communication that occur. Here we see that everyone is greeted personally and this includes the child. Even if there was a very young baby in a pram the therapist would make a point of trying to have some direct interaction with the infant. If there was an elderly person, this person would be greeted with the respect that is due to them. If someone attends the meeting who is unknown to the therapist, a polite therapist should say 'I'm not sure who you are?'. In doing this it is necessary to clarify the relationship between this person and those present in the room. In our example above the therapist very early on finds a way of identifying aspects of the relationship of those concerned where she talks about the 'Mum and Dad'. Some family therapists would be keen to use first names as soon as possible so that the defining role of 'mother' or 'father' can be expanded rather than seen as limiting 'who the full person is'.

In this example we also see that the first person to be greeted is the first person who enters the room. This person has a role of 'trailblazer' and in this sense acts as a leader and protector for all those who follow. If a child runs into the room first the therapist might prefer to greet the first adult and turn to the child later. This gives a clear message that the adults will speak first together and hold the executive subsystem position.

The example also demonstrates how the therapist will immediately comment on the behaviour that occurs in the room. The parents don't sit next to each other: they take seats apart, which means that the child has to sit between them. The therapist notices this and makes some seeming 'small talk' about what is happening. So even in the process of meeting the individuals, the therapist is outlining the communication process that will occur for them all.

22

Explaining the process

Everybody will have had the experience of attending for an appointment with a health professional and telling them the story about why they are attending. This is the template that family members bring to a first session with a family therapist. Sometimes this story can be like a tidal wave: family members (often one) desperate to help the therapist understand the whole story. At other times there might be a reticence to speak. So right from the outset the therapist needs to control how the story is told and explain how the process of therapy will go. This may involve a little bit of a speech right at the beginning, but this is still helpful in gaining everybody's attention and in teaching family members that taking turns in talking and listening will be a fundamental part of what is to happen.

> *Therapist:* Well it's nice to meet you all. As I said I work here as a therapist and what I do is to meet with families to talk about their problems and worries as I know that there isn't a family that doesn't have some kind of problem or some kind of worry. The way I do this is to let everybody tell me what they think is happening so we have something to talk about. But first I need to tell you what has happened that's got you into seeing me today just so that we can all be clear. I had a letter from your GP in which he tells me that Mrs Jones has been along to see him on two or three occasions as you have been concerned about Robert's behaviour (*looks at Mrs Jones, who nods back*). Your GP tells me that Mrs Jones finds Robert's behaviour difficult at times and that she thinks he doesn't listen to her very

much. He told me that the school have also complained that they don't know how to help Robert. He also told me that he's not met you Mr Jones to talk about this issue (*looks at Mr Jones, who nods back*), but he did tell me that Mr Jones has been along to see him because of high blood pressure and feeling very stressed at work.

Mr Jones: Oh I didn't think that had anything to do with Rob's behaviour.

Therapist: Well it may or may not and at some point we may find out the answer to that if it seems to be important. But at the moment I'm not sure whether Robert knows about the reason why he has come along today (*looks at the boy*) but it does seem Rob as if some people find it hard to manage and understand what you get up to and this is going to make life difficult for you and everyone around you. So that's how come we're all here today – so how can I help?

In explaining the process the therapist finds a way of linking each individual in some personal way to the process that has led to the session taking place. The therapist does not hold back on any information she has been given and is quite open about what contacts and communications have taken place prior to everyone meeting.

It is also important for the therapist to establish certain 'ground rules' about the conversation they are about to have. These will include the professional responsibility of the therapist to act if she thinks an individual is at risk or is vulnerable, but may also include with whom the therapist might share the outcomes of the conversation: with the referrer (in this case the GP), with her team or with her supervisor.

23

Listening to the story

The usual family response to 'how can I help?' is for the family spokesperson to provide an account of the difficulty, typically intermingled with some history. This account will probably have been rehearsed mentally. Moreover, other family members will have certainly heard elements of it, though not necessarily in the version that is given on this occasion. Everyone in the room knows this bit of the interview will happen and it is likely that it will follow a predictable pattern that will fit particular family rules. At this stage it may not be possible for the therapist to identify what these rules are, but she should mentally record any that become noticeable. One such classic family rule would be that the mother or father always begins the process of relating to outside professionals. Another might be that interactions begin with a criticism (e.g. 'It's all Robert's fault'). Some therapists will seek to delay the discussion of the 'story' with a view to having some 'problem-free talk', but usually the family will know they have come to the session for help and will soon assert the need to talk about the problem. The therapist needs to listen, clarify essential details as they arise and essentially be a recipient of the information.

Mrs Jones: I went back to work about nine months ago and since that time Rob has been more of a handful. At least I think so and I'm not sure if Rob resents me not being there all the time as he has to go to his grandmother's after school. My husband thinks the problems are not that big and it's all in my mind and of course he's got his own difficulties to worry about because work is not going very well. It just seems as if we've got a lot on at the present time and Rob's behaviour does seem

> to make everything worse. I'm sure we would
> manage quite well if Rob wasn't so difficult.

The therapist's response to this would be some straightforward paraphrasing and summarising of what Mrs Jones said, with the essential element being 'okay this is how I understand it at the moment' but with the 'but of course things can change' very much in parentheses. With this beginning story it is possible that there will be interruptions and the like, and the therapist will need to use some clear structuring skills to ensure that one story is given in totality as this will provide the content around which further conversations will take place. So in our example we might find a therapist saying (with other family members talking over Mrs Jones): *'Please, one at a time. I'll give everybody a chance. I think it would be helpful if we let Mrs Jones finish and I know now that you have a different view Mr Jones but we'll check out other views once we've got her telling clear and finished.'*

The therapist also needs to establish continuity with the previous work by asking how the referral process linked in to what was happening in the family (*'So how did you decide to go to see the GP because of the problem?'*). The therapist therefore structures the session further by allowing a telling of the story of the problem, by indicating that everybody will have their opportunity to express their perception and will link this to what has gone on before so that there is a historical connection between what happened outside of the session and what is happening inside the session.

There are two ideas that family therapists have emphasised in this initial stage of the interview (Minuchin 1974; Haley 1976). The first is that the therapist should notice any significant 'phrases of language' that are used by the family. For instance, in the example Mrs Jones talks about Rob 'resenting' her because she has gone back to work. This is a use of language that the therapist needs to hear and remember. It both represents a 'meaning' ascribed to the behaviour of Rob and it gives the therapist the opportunity to develop the interactional nature of the problem description. So the therapist might respond with 'So Mrs Jones, you think that going back to work has encouraged

Rob to show his anger'. The second idea used in this early stage of therapy is to 'test the water' with a number of alternative ideas and descriptions. In this process, by hearing feedback, the therapist will discover which ideas fit best for the family. Thus the above description about Rob's anger allows the therapist to see if the word 'encourage' was well received. The therapist might then say 'So Rob's expression of anger is his way of saying he is hurting, and missing his Mum'. Such a description immediately lessens the criticism of Rob and connects his response to his Mum's behaviour. What family therapists are looking for here is language that 'loosens' the system's definition of the problem.

24

Capturing everyone's perspective

Even though families may have talked about a problem for a considerable period of time it is quite likely that they have not had the experience of hearing someone else respond to their difficulty from a neutral position. If they have ever had a conversation with friends or other professionals, it is quite likely that there was an unwitting attempt to have that person see the problem from the perspective of the person doing the telling. It is as if we all naturally want somebody to say to us 'yes you are right' and join our campaign against the others (whoever they may be).

To some extent this is to recognise that when we live in intimate relationships with other people, conflict or difference is inevitable as it is not possible for everyone to see the world in the same way. Even though we would all like somebody to agree fully with our viewpoint, taking sides is not helpful in the therapeutic process with families. The aim for the therapist is to allow everybody to say how they perceive the situation and for everybody to notice that the therapist is someone who can accept that there is difference between family members. The therapist needs to convey the message that she is interested in everyone's view and she expects everyone to have a view: '*So Mrs Jones that's how you see the problem; Mr Jones is that how the problem looks for you?*'

At this point the answers may range from complete agreement 'yes that's exactly how it looks for us both' to a complete disagreement. Mr Jones might say that he does not believe that the boy has a problem or that the problem is something that will 'sort itself out' or even that he did not agree with coming to meet the therapist. Whatever is said, the therapist will find it necessary to prevent family members arguing or switching off as they hear each other's point of view. One of the defining skills of an interactive approach is the ability to paraphrase and summarise on statements made by two people and to maintain the attention and involvement of those that have different views: *'Okay, so your husband says it happens this way but you think it happens in a different way. For you Mrs Jones the problem is the way in which Robert is dealing with you not being there and for Mr Jones it sometimes seems as if there is not a problem but just Mrs Jones worrying.'*

Not only is it important to allow the adults to state the way in which they see the problem, but the children should also be asked a question about the nature of the difficulty as it seems to them. Obviously this question will vary depending on the age of the children. Adolescents are best treated in an almost adult manner, with the younger children being asked questions in a more age appropriate way. Some family therapists would suggest that children should be brought into the conversation after the adults have spoken as this emphasises that adults are responsible for family life and, by inference, for working together to solve family problems. The therapist, in this early stage, is helping the family see that hearing *difference* is itself one of the key processes in family therapy. Thus, although the phase when everyone talks from their own perspective might seem laborious with a family of six members, this is the foundation of the change process itself.

25

Asking and empathy

To help the family discover new information, the therapist is simply asking questions at this point in the therapeutic process. The questions she asks are about how individuals think, feel and behave and how groups of individuals interact. The therapist therefore asks questions *of the system* so that the information produced will reveal the way the family is interconnected and how it operates as a system. As this information is generated, the family should begin to become aware of their way of inter-acting. The therapist's practical aim is to question in a way that releases new information for the family to consider. This aware-ness should help family members reach a new understanding, which can then lead to change.

Questions are therefore asked in a way that sets family members thinking, both individually and collectively, about the implications of their answers. The questions are not designed to reveal 'facts' but to create a chain of reflective thought in which the interconnectedness of the family as a system becomes apparent to its members. It is usually not helpful for the ther-apist to ask leading questions (to which she knows the answer) but rather to ask questions whose effect and answer are deter-mined by the client. The intentions and actions of the therapist serve only to trigger a response; they do not determine it. The questions serve as a way of having people think about what they do and what they do with respect to others. They invite every-one to be reflective about their own actions and about their actions in the system. By encouraging this kind of reflective thinking the questions have the effect of creating 'reflexivity' in the system itself (Tomm 1988). (Specific types of questions are discussed fully in Points 49–55.)

The stance that is most useful at this stage is a commonality of all therapies, that of non-judgemental active listening (Kirschenbaum and Henderson 1990; O'Leary 1999). The family therapist will need to be able to demonstrate empathy and acceptance in order to facilitate this process. Empathy is essential for engaging individuals in honest and full participation in family therapy. The therapist's empathic response encourages family members to express long felt, but incompletely understood and seldom voiced, aspects of their experience. Empathy is therefore a tool for understanding, this being achieved by reflection of feeling and open receptive listening. In offering empathic responses the fact that more than one person is present in the room presents a problem of a different order compared with individual therapy. Every family member is watchful of the therapist's acceptance of his or her self, of the acceptance of other individuals and of the acceptance of the family as a whole. Once family members feel understood and accepted by the presence of a receptive listener, they acquire a sense of security and strength that allows them to declare their own desires and to be receptive to what others in the family want (see Point 26).

26

The therapeutic alliance

What we have been describing in the last few points has been variously labelled the 'common skills' or 'common factors' of all therapies as they are applied to family therapy (Hubble *et al.* 2000; Safran and Muran 2000; Friedlander *et al.* 2006). Research confirms that these factors account for a large element of the success of therapy (Hubble *et al.* 2000). When these factors are not rated highly by families, moreover, they account for high dropout rates (Friedlander *et al.* 2006). A number of theoreticians and researchers have termed these factors the 'therapeutic alliance' (Flaskas and Perlesz 1996). This is defined as the relationship between the client(s) and the therapist in relation to the therapy that needs to be undertaken. In studies of individual therapy this construct has been divided into a number of elements that usually include the 'bond' between therapist and client(s), the level of agreement about the tasks of the therapy and a willingness to work towards the goals of the therapy. In family therapy, the therapeutic alliance is clearly more complicated than the alliance in individual therapy. For instance, in family therapy, the alliance needs to be understood as relating to both the whole family in relation to the therapist as well as in relation to each individual family member relating to the therapist. A further complexity is that each family member will almost certainly vary in their commitment, understanding and willingness to change, in relation to the therapeutic task. Family therapists (Friedlander *et al.* 2006) currently describe this concept as consisting of four dimensions: *(a) the emotional connection with the therapist, (b) engagement in the therapeutic process, (c) safety within the therapeutic system and (d) a shared sense of purpose within the family.* Of these four dimensions, two (emotional connection and engagement in therapy) are shared with all other therapeutic interventions. The other two are unique to family therapy as this form of therapy elicits the need for family members to feel safe when talking in front of each other and to share a view that therapy together can be helpful.

The value of understanding the role of the therapeutic alliance in family therapy is that it highlights the kinds of behaviour that can be helpful in developing a better alliance between therapist and family. The developers of the current alliance research (Friedlander *et al.* 2006) suggest that certain therapist behaviour is more likely to increase the alliance whilst others are likely to diminish it. In the previous points we have described a number of therapist behaviours that will increase the therapeutic alliance, such as listening carefully to each family member (increases emotional bond to therapist), explaining what family therapy is about (increases shared sense of purpose) and capturing everybody's perspective (increases sense of safety). It equally gives ideas about what behaviours might not be so helpful, therefore, a therapist should be mindful that too much negative discussion might make family members feel less safe and therefore not want to come to therapy. If we return to an example we used in an earlier point, an open, respectful response will allow Mr Jones to air his views but in a safe way.

Mr Jones: I think my wife is just making too much of a deal about Rob at present.

Therapist: So I understand that you think your wife is more worried than you are about Rob. Do you have an idea about why she should be more worried than you?

Attention to the therapeutic alliance literature raises a number of important aspects for family therapy practice. The first is that often families will rate the alliance lower than the therapist (e.g. therapists have a tendency to view their work through 'rose coloured spectacles'). Secondly, the global family rating of the alliance is significant but differences between family members can be more significant. For instance, in the Jones family, if the husband continued to feel negatively about being in therapy whilst his wife continued to feel safe and positive, this would be *more* likely to lead to a poor outcome than if both shared an equivocal view of the therapy (Robbins *et al.* 2003).

Thirdly, of all the dimensions that seem most important in maintaining families in therapy, it is the emotional bond with the therapist that counts. Most therapists would want to establish that this 'emotional bond' is not to be associated with 'normal' relationships. Yet for families, 'liking' their therapist is clearly important and the most usual way for them to describe their therapist. This means that family therapists need to be respectful, amenable and socially competent.

Neutrality and the curious position

It has become customary for family therapists to describe their non-judgemental position with the words *neutrality* and *curiosity* (Palazzoli *et al.* 1980a; Cecchin 1987). Within families there are strong mechanisms that result in blame and guilt. A therapeutic way of interacting and talking to family members about their difficulty should not encourage these mechanisms even though they will often be very apparent. It is therefore important that the therapist, from the outset, works within a non-judgemental neutral position. This does not refer to an emotional non-involvement, e.g. an uncaring position. It refers to a *non-attachment* to the interactions, the stories, the feelings and the perspectives that all family members bring. The Milan school of family therapy (Palazzoli *et al.* 1980a) suggested that the therapist had 'got it right' if no family member thought that the therapist was 'on their side' (as opposed to other family members). Later ideas have suggested that this is best described as a *curious* stance because *neutrality* was being misconstrued as uncaring and would be inappropriate in situations where vulnerable family members need protection (Cecchin 1987). This means that the therapist is interested and even nosy about all the things that people imagine can occur. The therapist does not assume that she has grasped the meaning of even the common phrases that family members use to describe their lives; the therapist is interested in seeing how many different ways something can be described or explained rather than finding one 'right' description. This attitude to the evolving clinical material can be likened to the curiosity of an anthropologist (or ethnographer) who first meets a member of a new group.

Once more, from a family therapy perspective, this curiosity is part of the process of the therapy because it is contagious. When the family therapist asks Mr Jones why he thinks his wife has the views she does, the therapist hopes to arise curiosity in all family members, not just herself! By holding out the possibility of a wide range of thinking, feeling and behaving that is possible in this and any family, the therapist is attempting to help family members move away from their standard ways of responding to the current situation. By being curious, the therapist can make apparent a multitude of possible descriptions of one interaction; hence one description does not become the 'truth' as it is possible for any one piece of interaction to be described in a variety of ways. The therapist is not seeking the 'best' description or the most 'suitable' description from the 'most able' family member. The therapist is just interested in the variety of ways in which anything can be described and is curious about how different people see circumstances and their emotional and cognitive responses to those circumstances.

The therapist is interested and wishes to help the family see how the possible descriptions they have arrived at fit together and what descriptions might be useful for change now and in the future. The more curious or inquisitive a therapist is, the more the family have an opportunity to think about their own interaction.

Different families will experience the neutral position differently and the therapist needs to be mindful of this. Sometimes families find the curious stance odd: They have come expecting an 'expert' to tell them what to do. In such situations, the therapist may need to explain why she asks the questions she does and why she wants to stimulate the family to find a solution that works for them (and not necessarily for other families). She may also want to say that staying curious keeps the family working hard during the therapy session: They may be curious about what kind of questions will come next.

28

Reflection of feeling

Empathy is also demonstrated by the therapist letting family members know that she understands their experience by reflection of the feelings expressed in the session. This affirms the individual's experience and at the same time intensifies the awareness of it, so that a feeling of authenticity is experienced. This type of reflection provides feedback to one person about what one person understands another person is feeling. Hence it also serves as a means by which the therapist can check out her perceptions of the client's position. It is, therefore, a process by which an individual's internal frame of reference is clarified within the context of firstly a relationship to the therapist and secondly within the context of the relationship to the other family members who are observing the therapist reflecting the feeling of that particular individual. For the therapist it begins with thinking and feeling with the individual, that is, a focus on the 'I' of the individual, and this then moves to thinking and feeling about the individual in context; initially this is a focus on the relationship between the therapist and the individual, a focus on the 'me and you'. The systemic therapist goes on to encourage the individual to consider the 'me – us' dimension by ensuring that other family members are asked questions on that particular issue. This process of reflecting on feelings links the experience of individual family members to a collaborative, but often unexpressed, 'us' dimension of interaction. Each individual therefore hears a reflection of his or her own statements and reflections of the statements of others. Thus a typical reflection of feeling sequence will be:

Therapist:	Asks a question of A.
A:	Answers.
Therapist:	Reflects the feeling from A.
	Asks B about A's answer.

B:	Answers.
Therapist:	Reflects feeling from B.
	Asks A about B's answer.

For example:

Therapist:	Mrs Smith when your daughter argues with her father what is it like for you?
Mrs Smith:	It is very difficult. I end up crying.
Therapist:	You become tearful?
Mrs Smith:	Yes I just feel helpless, miserable and I can't do anything to stop it.
Therapist:	So you feel inadequate and sad that you can't prevent it?
Mrs Smith:	Yes that's about it.
Therapist:	I was wondering Sheila (*daughter*), how does what your Mum says make you feel?
Sheila:	I know it makes Mum sad but I can't help that, the argument just takes over.
Therapist:	So even though you know how it makes your Mum feel you're overwhelmed by the angry feelings so that you can't attend to other things?
Sheila:	Yes I suppose that's right.
Therapist:	Do you think you're good at other times at recognising when your Mum is sad?

Through the process of reflection of feeling the therapist therefore firstly connects to an individual. This occurs in a way that allows the individual to connect to herself. The process of questioning then connects family members to each other. In the example above, Sheila is connected to her mother because of the feeling of her mother. But also as Mr Smith is present, he is observing what is occurring and so his connection to daughter and his wife is present in his mind and in the mind of the other family members. Hence the multitude of emotional ways in which family members are connected to each other is brought out into the open by this simple process of questioning and reflecting the feeling of all involved.

29

Reflection of interaction

As the reflection of feeling links the experience of several family members the interactive process emerges as the questioning continues. The therapist adds to the reflection of feeling by then reflecting back short sequences of interaction that may have occurred in the session or, more likely, would have been reported on by family members. In this manner the therapist is therefore focusing on emotional reactions and behavioural interactions. An example best illustrates the process of reflection of interaction.

Therapist: Mrs Smith, when your daughter argues with her father what do you do?

Mrs Smith: I try and stop them.

Therapist: How do you do that?

Mrs Smith: I say 'please stop' and then I tell Sheila to leave it lie, to let things be.

Therapist: So you want them to stop, you ask them both first but then you concentrate on getting Sheila to give it up?

Mrs Smith: Yes, that's right.

Therapist: Is that how you see things going Sheila? Is that what happens for you?

Sheila: Well I think that Dad starts it, you know getting on at me and then I get on at him. Mum then tells us to stop arguing; she actually tries to get in between us but she always blames me, tells me it's my fault.

Therapist: So your experience is that your Dad starts to have a go at you and you have a go back. Your mother comes in to try to stop it, mainly by telling you that it's your fault. Let's see if I can put all this together; the argument starts, Sheila thinks her father started it. I'm guessing you're not there Mrs Smith but you hear it. You come to where they are shouting at each other. You then stand between Sheila and her father but then you say a number of things mainly to Sheila. Mrs Smith you see yourself just telling her to stop and Sheila, you see yourself being told off. (*Mrs Smith and Sheila both nod.*) So Mrs Smith what are you feeling now that Sheila says she thinks you are telling her off?

Here we can see the basic structure of the reflection of interaction sequence:

Therapist:	Asks a question of A.
A:	Answers.
Therapist:	Reflects interaction from A's reply.
	Asks a question of B.
B:	Answers.
Therapist:	Reflects interaction from B's reply.
	Reflects interaction from A and B replies.
	Questions continue.

Reflection of interaction sequences encourage the family to move beyond individual frames of reference to the interactions that link these frames of reference. By talking about interactions in this way the therapist is able to show her caring for the family while at the same time exhibiting a distance (a neutrality) from their interactive processes. In this way each individual in the family is able to hear reflections on how they individually interact with each other and on how they as a family interact. Sometimes, the therapist might draw these interactive cycles on a piece of paper or white board. This demonstrates in a visible manner the circularities of family interaction.

30

Tracking interactions

From the family's view the problem they are encountering is limited to a particular set of behaviours and interactions. The family systems view, however, considers that any reported problem is contained within a much wider interactive pattern than that considered by the family. The notion used to explain this is that of '*punctuation of interaction*'. In families each group of interactions is separated from others with a beginning and an ending. Much as with writing a sentence: you start with a capital letter and end with a full stop. Punctuating words in this way gives a particular meaning to the words in the sentence and distinguishes it from other sentences. However, the systems view is that life is just a continual stream of interaction (the words) and that where one places the beginning and end (the capital letter or full stop) is arbitrary. Each means of punctuating interaction makes sense in its own right. Hence, how we begin to consider a group of interactions may result in them having a different meaning depending on where we start or even finish. The notion of punctuation implies that any observable behaviour is part of a larger pattern of interaction (much as the field example in Point 1). The therapist therefore has the task of exploring the interactive element of any reported problem and expanding the length of that interactive sequence so that the family can, in their own way, arrive at their own new punctuation. To do this the family need help in appreciating how the problem is embedded in how they interact.

The therapist selects and is often led by the family to consider instances of the problem and, from that, works backwards and forwards in time so that the full sequence of events can be appreciated. The therapist is helped by the family as nearly all the spontaneous reporting that is done by family members tends to be interactive shorthand: '*I tell her to stop and she doesn't but shouts back at me.*' Such a report is a statement of how the interaction should be viewed but it does not convey all the information that is necessary to a curious observer. One of the reasons why the family will be stuck with this problem is that there is an acceptance of this way of punctuating what happens whereas a more closely observed version will contain more choice points where a difference could potentially occur.

Therapist:	Sheila you said that your Dad just seems to pick on you. Is this at any particular time?
Sheila:	It tends to be early in the evening; he will be sitting down and Mum will be in the kitchen clearing things up after tea.
Therapist:	So what are you doing?
Sheila:	I may have helped Mum a bit or I may be just leaving the kitchen, perhaps doing the same as him.
Therapist:	So Dad has left the kitchen after teatime and you follow, with Mum staying in the kitchen. Is that what happens before the argument starts?
Sheila:	Yes that's what happens and he usually says something about me not helping Mum but then says something else that he thinks I've done wrong, like coming home late the other evening.
Therapist:	So is it just about you helping your mother in the kitchen or is it usually about something else that you start to argue?
Sheila:	Most of the time it is about something else, as if he is just using the business with doing some housework as an excuse to get at me about something else that will have happened earlier on.
Therapist:	Mrs Smith, do you know that is what the argument is about?
Mrs Smith:	I usually know if he is angry about something to do with her because he has told me, but I never know if he is going to say something.

Therapist: So Mr Smith will have told you about something quite a time before the argument that you were not sure was going to happen?

Mrs Smith: Yes and I suppose I'm waiting for it in some way.

Therapist: As we work backwards from the argument I'm wondering if you are beginning to see some connections here?

In this example, the therapist is tracking the claimed 'argument' but is finding historical 'punctuations' that seem as relevant as the event itself.

31

Establishing the family ideology

In order to deal with the amount of information that is all around us in social relationships, we each develop ways of categorising that information and linking the categories together so that in some way they organise and predict how our world will work. We use our own categories or constructs to build up a view of how the social world is happening for us. By placing psychological order in our world we not only simply organise it but we actively create it, in such a way that future events are seen as fitting in with the organisation that we have placed on the world. It therefore becomes possible for us to deal with future time by predicting how we believe social events occur and how people will behave. The way in which we shape our information becomes an 'ideology' – a system of psychological categories and constructs that shape and provide meaning for how we think about our experience in the world (Street and Downey 1996).

For two people to interact effectively they do not necessarily need to work according to the same constructs but they should have some constructs about how each other sees the world. So not only do we have a theory about the world from our perspective but in order to relate to another person we include in our theory a view about the perspective of the other (Dallos 1997). The constructs that individuals have, be they shared or otherwise, embody the meaning of how interaction and behaviour from the past and present are viewed, as well as providing information about what action is necessary for the future. Some meanings are shared and others are held by individuals, and together they form a whole that determines how the individuals interact. It is this whole that constitutes the 'family ideology' – the family set of meanings about their social world.

As the ideology is helpful in determining how the future is to be dealt with, it therefore contains the rules about how relationships and interactions should occur. The word ideology refers to a particular set of constructs about actual behaviour and personal values and ideals; it implies an organised body of ideas that reflect the beliefs of the individuals that make up the family. Beliefs about how people will behave in any particular set of circumstances are the most important ones. An ideology therefore not only tells us how an individual or a family thinks and reacts about particular situations but it also gives an indication of how that situation will be evaluated in terms of self-preservation, and the meeting of ideals and values. This set of meanings provides the foundation of the cognitive dimension for how people behave in any particular situation.

In terms of the problem for which the family attend there will be a family ideology about the problem; each individual will have an ideology about the perspective of others and they each will have an ideology about the perspective of others on the problem. The therapist therefore has the task of assisting the family in communicating about the meaning they ascribe to their problems. The basic question to ask is '*how do you think this came to happen?*' and by asking this she is trying to identify those areas where they have a shared view and those in which they are in conflict. She will be investigating with them the cohesiveness and the differences in their family ideology. As the meanings are revealed, the basis for moving towards negotiations for solutions becomes a possibility.

Therapist:	Mrs Jones, you explained to me how Robert won't do what you ask of him and how he seems to be distancing himself from you. As you think about it, what sort of explanations do you have for this happening?
Mrs Jones:	I think he doesn't like the fact that I'm not available any more and he's getting his own back on me.
Therapist:	So that seems to make you sad. Do you have any ideas about changing things?
Mrs Jones:	I know it's difficult and I wondered if I should give up my job. But then if he could accept it, things would be different and if he

	could get used to other people doing things for him I'm sure they would help.
Therapist:	So does that mean for you there's a choice between you giving up or somebody spending a lot of time with him?
Mrs Jones:	Yes it does and that seems to be a very difficult choice to make.
Therapist:	And do you think you're the only person who sees that choice or are there others in the family who also see that?
Mrs Jones:	No I expect myself to deal with this as I decided to go back to work myself.
Therapist:	So Mr Jones what are your thoughts and feelings about what your wife has just said?

The therapist now has a good idea about the ideology that underpins how Mrs Jones sees the problem and its solution. Of course this ideology also relates to societal ideologies such as 'mothers are responsible for their children (not fathers)' and 'mothers who go back to work affect their children's development'. The therapist may choose later to loosen the descriptive power of these, but at present is seeking alternative ideologies within the family to see if other ideas might offer better options.

32

Children and play

It is highly likely that some aspect of family work will involve younger children and so particular arrangements need to be put in place to include the way in which they behave and communicate. The creation of a 'child friendly' atmosphere is of course important in any setting in which children are involved. This includes having pictures and decorations on the wall that the child can relate to and having child-sized furniture and appropriate play material so that the children are given a very clear message that their presence is very much wished and wanted (e.g. children are seen *and* heard). This allows children to relax and to relate to what is going on in an unpressured way. Drawing materials and dolls houses with small sets of doll families are a valuable addition to any consulting room, but it is helpful if there is not *too* much play material as this can create too much distraction for some children.

Young children communicate their thoughts and feelings through the activity of their play. At varying times in family sessions they may produce something that has relevance to the themes being discussed, so their contribution to family work is essential. Children can often signal important themes and events by making direct verbal statements or communicating something by their play. The therapist will, at times, need to link the themes being discussed with what the child is expressing in its play. The child's perspective is important not in any dominating or patronising way but just as one other perspective (Wilson 1998). At other times the therapist will be able to direct the child's activity by suggesting that they draw a picture of the events that the parents are talking about or that they act out the event with the small dolls available. This can also help to slow down the discussion of parents and include the children's voice.

It is important that the therapist has good communication skills with children (Wilson 1998) and these are skills that will always be exhibited within the context of their parents being present. This poses challenges. The therapist does not want to appear to be so good at being in the child's world that the parents feel less competent as parents. The preference is therefore to encourage parents to talk to their children as much as the therapist does.

33

Observation of interaction in the room

Families do not interact in a random fashion. Their interactions follow patterns that have been set up over a period of time and these patterns will emerge in the therapy room. The therapy situation itself provides a 'task' for the family to perform and their usual interactions in problem-solving situations will come into force. Thus *how* the family interact will have some bearing on the way they interact about the problem that brought them to therapy and it will inform the therapist of their general interactive style. It is quite probable that certain interactions observed in the room will be similar to the interactions that are significant in maintaining the problem.

In the initial phases of therapy the therapist needs to be aware of these types of interactive patterns:

Who comes in the room first? Who helps the children to settle down and who provides instructions to the children? How do the family arrange their sitting? Do couples sit next to each other or do they allow someone to sit between them? Who begins talk about the problem and how do other people deal with their listening role? Who interrupts who and how does one person deal with being interrupted? If the therapist makes a mistake by getting someone's name wrong or suggesting that something happened that didn't happen, who is the person that corrects the therapist? When two family members have a discussion, who is the person that stops the discussion and involves someone else and who is the someone else that they involve? Do the children become more active when a particular emotional theme arises? How do the children 'interfere' with the adults' interaction and is it when a particular sequence of events occurs?

Certainly in the initial session, and perhaps even in the second session, it is too early to comment on the similarity between the interactions in the therapy room and the reported patterns as they occur elsewhere. But the therapist needs to be mindful and note patterns because at some stage these will be important to feed back to the family. However, from the outset the therapist will need to let the family know that she will make comments about what happens in the room and, importantly, that she will at some time make a link between events inside and outside the room, which serves to help the family become more aware of the means by which they interact: '*I noticed just then that when you and your wife were talking about the children's behaviour your daughter kept interrupting you. Is that what happens at home?*'

As there is so much interaction and information being generated within the family therapy session it is difficult for the therapist to notice everything that is occurring. Even very experienced therapists often miss significant interactions. It is for this reason that family therapists have made use of a number of techniques to improve the 'watching' – one-way screens so that colleagues can observe, video recordings made for post session viewing and also having a co-therapist in the room who serves as an observer. For some therapists these approaches are merely ways of having more pairs of eyes observe what is going on. Other therapists have developed them into specific techniques that make use of the observer 'outside' the room having a specific input (see Point 98).

34

Establishing the family's position regarding therapy

Individuals and families do not come to therapy with a clear worked-out view of what will happen. Few people have the expectation: 'I thought that we would talk about things and slowly I would have a different feeling about the problem and then constructively build some alternative strategies for dealing with it.' Few of us when we have troubles, worries and distress think that clearly. However, family members will have thought about what will happen during therapy ever since the appointment was made. There may be several elements to these thoughts. First, there may be 'magical thinking' that somehow the therapist will raise a magic wand and everything will suddenly become different. Though most people are able to realise that thoughts of this nature are unrealistic, it is important, early on in therapy, to acknowledge that this may be what family members hope for. We can see that such a magical wish may be connected to family members feeling defeated by their problems and wanting someone else to solve them for them. Secondly, many children will come to therapy expecting a 'telling off' and more worryingly may fear being 'taken from their family' or medically examined in some way. One of the authors once met a family where the child had been told he was coming to the dentist! In his case he was expecting something very different from what he got. Other expectations might be related to those emotions underlying the problem, that is, that 'blame' and 'responsibility' will be portioned out by the therapist.

Not only will these thoughts and feelings be present but family members may have specific expectations as to how the therapist may behave. Since we know that the therapist must collaborate on joint goals with families for the therapy to be successful (Friedlander *et al.* 2006), it is important that the therapist attend to these expectations as well. It may be useful to begin with the question: '*What were you expecting to happen today when you met me? What were you expecting me to do?*'

This is the beginning of the negotiation process between the family and the professional about the tasks of therapy. Street and Downey (1996) have identified particular family responses to this standard question:

Reluctant customers:	We only came because we were sent.
Action expected:	We thought you would be doing something about this.
Opinion seekers:	We want your opinion on what is wrong.
Advice seekers:	We want you to tell us what to do.
Theory seekers:	We would like to understand why.
Therapy clients:	We thought that by talking about it we might sort something out.

In each case the therapist will be attempting to be as clear as possible about what the family expects. The most obvious follow-up question, once the family have stated what they are expecting to happen, will be: '*If I do this, how will it make a difference to how things happen in your family at the moment?*'

The answer to this question allows the collaborative process in setting therapy goals to begin. It also allows the therapist to understand how the family usually solve problems and to assess with them whether they need new methods or need to re-try old methods.

35

Feedback and providing summaries

At varying times over the course of the therapy sessions and within each session itself the therapist needs to provide the family with a summary feedback on what has been learnt or what has occurred over that particular time. The first aim in doing this is to check out with the family what the therapist's current understanding is and also to lay down the foundation for the therapeutic process that will go on from that time. It is helpful for the therapist to assume that at times she will not get the feedback correct and she should introduce a tentativeness to her statements. This can be achieved by using phrases like: '*I might have got this wrong, but it looks to me as if . . .*' Such tentativeness allows the family to construct a much more cohesive account of themselves *for themselves*. It is the ongoing construction of this narrative that maintains the family's sense of responsibility and active involvement in the therapy.

In the early phases of therapy it is important that the therapist feed back the family's narrative in terms of its historical development so that the family acquire more of a sense of their own process through time. Providing feedback in this way is helpful in that it begins the process of the family distinguishing between those events that occurred serendipitously, those events due to the actions of others and those due to the actions of themselves. It also allows for a logic to develop so that the family appreciate the actions they took themselves to remedy the problems and what future action, including work with the therapist, may be involved. The presentation of the narrative historically lays out the matter in a life cycle way and hence allows the family to consider what is happening to them within terms of the usual and normal processes that go on. Whenever giving such a summary it is important that each individual is mentioned in the narrative so that each can feel a part of the process.

In providing a summary, a therapist not only indicates her ability to listen and to convey to the family her willingness to see the problem from an agreed perspective but she is also able to point to issues that remain unclear and confusing. Through the process of a feedback summary the therapist can identify themes and issues that, because of their lack of clarity, require to be addressed in sessions. In many senses, the therapist conveys to the family that she sees her central task as being to continually offer such feedback as she elaborates her understanding of the family. This allows the family to see that they need to help the therapist understand. But this process also introduces an important element of uncertainty into the conversation: The therapist maintains a curious, inexact quality to her feedback by using terms like 'it might be that' or 'I am wondering if'.

As therapy progresses feedback summaries should always be provided at the beginning of every new session that recap what happened previously. This is then connected to what has happened between sessions.

36

Considering external systemic pressures

The vagaries of life and the perpetual changing nature of the world throw up expected and unexpected events that all families have to deal with. Families display a wide range of adaptations to similar events and clearly nothing can be labelled as stressful unless it is perceived as such by family members. Stress is only identified when individuals believe that any given situation will place demands on themselves that will tax or exceed the resources available to them (Street and Rivett 1996). Stress is not equivalent to the triggering event or the circumstances surrounding that event, nor is it something that resides within an individual. Stress is the result of an interaction between an individual or a family and the circumstances in which they find themselves. Stress is therefore contextual and the context in which families find themselves can, at times, contain a considerable amount of pressure. It is therefore important not to label particular families who are struggling with problems as having their own internal difficulties when, in fact, it is in many respects just a response to an overwhelming external stress that is effecting the family.

An example of such a traumatic external pressure would be when a family therapist is asked to work with families who are refugees from war or economic deprivation. Some families, under these conditions, could have met with violent and abusive events that affect the way in which they view themselves (Woodcock 2001). Other families could be living in situations of exceptionally high social disadvantage with unsuitable educational opportunities for their children, and they may have to confront high crime rates and unemployment. As such the effect of poverty can be considerable on families (Minuchin *et al.* 1998). Families of minority ethnic groups experience forms of racism within many cultures (Boyd-Franklin 2003) that have major effects on their daily life. These are all types of wider situations that can affect how a family function, particularly in terms of how they parent children and care for the elderly.

Certainly in engaging any family a therapist must be aware of the existence and the effect of external systemic pressures. The position of curiosity is one that the therapist must use to investigate the environmental difficulties that the family face.

'What is it like living in that area?'
'How have you settled into this country after your move?'
'How do you manage the money to ensure that everybody gets everything that they need?'
'How do you get on with your children's school?'

There are specific interventions and ways of helping families that have confronted major disruptions and social upheavals. In all cases the aim is to work with the family by focusing on their strengths and helping them develop a resilience towards the difficulties that they have faced. An important aspect of this, as with any type of therapy, is the engendering of hope that life can be different and fulfilling.

37

Family resilience

In order to deal with the world that is forever changing and can and will throw up difficulties, families need to have the ability to mobilise their own resources to deal with the problems that will arise for them. All families will face crises when the usual pattern of life is disrupted and when they need to respond in a way that they are not necessarily used to and they have had little experience of in the past. In order to manage these situations, families require a resilience: an ability to deal with difficult situations; bouncing back; and then continuing in a way in which all family members maintain their sense of integrity and fulfilment. There are certain qualities in families that promote this resilience. In therapy the therapist will note the qualities the family has and will try to enhance them as the therapeutic process continues.

The features of resilient families are (Walsh 1998, 2003):

- **Good communication**. This is when communication is open, honest, positive and where family members communicate with each other frequently.
- **A sense of togetherness**. This is the feeling of being a part of something that helps to bond a family and give members a sense of belonging. An important aspect of this is the sharing of similar values, beliefs and morals.
- **Sharing activities**. Resilient families share a variety of activities together that invariably include having meals together and sharing leisure time together in some way.
- **Showing affection**. The demonstration of love, care, concern and interest for each other on a regular basis helps to increase a sense of connection within strong positive emotions.
- **Active support**. This involves assisting, encouraging and reassuring each other. Families are seen as being resilient

when everyone feels equally comfortable in offering or asking for support.

- **Acceptance**. Families need to show respect, understanding and appreciation for one another's individuality and uniqueness. It is the respectful recognition of difference that allows a family to act in a cohesive way.

- **Commitment**. There needs to be a clear sense of dedication and loyalty to the family as a whole, with family members showing a strong desire to be a part of this family and recognising that the 'Us' is more important than the 'Me'.

As these qualities assist the family in dealing with all sorts of problems, the aim in any therapeutic endeavour is not just to stimulate these in order to deal with the current problem, but to stimulate communication, sharing, acceptance, etc. so that the family can deal with other problems that may befall them in future.

38

Investigating the family supportive network

Families are embedded in a range of other systems and are in fact subsystems of much larger social groupings/networks. It is evident that families benefit from the social support they receive from these networks that they construct around themselves. When a family faces problems it draws on this network to help deal with difficulties. In the case of a crisis, the family system not only draws from sources of support that it already has, but will seek additional forms of support. This network may help a family in a number of ways, by providing emotional support (knowing someone cares about your trouble), esteem support (knowing someone values your attempts) and information support (giving ideas that may help).

The social network will include:

1 The extended family: The type of involvement will be very variable, ranging from babysitting and child minding to looking after the elderly and going on holiday together. For some it will involve no contact at all.

2 Educational services: As children spend so much time in school the networks that are created in and around the educational setting are very important. These also include preschool provisions and after school clubs. This network provides a way for children to make contact with other children and also for parents meeting other parents. Some professional staff in schools are exceptionally helpful to parents when they are faced with a difficulty.

3 Religious and community groups: Families vary in the way they become involved in activities in the community. Some certainly define aspects of their identity by their membership of such groups. These groups can give family members different opportunities to discuss problematic matters and at times they may provide practical help.

4   Work colleagues and friends: The network of acquaintances that the family constructs through its history and its daily life also provides a resource for help and sustenance to family members.

5   Professional agencies: Nearly all families meeting difficulties will have some contact with a professional agency. The way in which such professional 'helpers' manage their role and the resources that they are able to offer can have a significant impact on how a family manages a particular difficult situation.

Each family will have a very unique network and a unique way of connecting to this network. The therapist needs to be able to track the extent of the network and the nature of the connection between family and network. It is important to do this because there may be conflicts as well as support within this connection. One family member may find an aspect of their social network very helpful and supportive whereas another might find it to be intrusive or not helpful (this is often the case in dealing with extended family). Consequently potential supports can sometimes have a divisive effect on families. Similarly professional agencies such as schools or social services departments can create extra pressures on the family. Although the range of support from outside the family can be limitless, when a therapist meets a family she should fully investigate what activities are helpful and what are not.

'Who are you most in contact with?'
'Who helps you most with this?'
'Did you find that professional x offered you a lot of help? How could what he did have been more helpful?'

39

Setting the therapy agenda

An essential task in the first if not the second session is for the therapist to outline an agenda for what is to be discussed and how sessions will be arranged. It is likely that in the initial phases the therapist will have led the discussion to some areas that the family did not expect and that the discussion has been wider ranging than they had anticipated. However, in forming an agreed agenda it is the presenting problem – placed in its interactional context – that constitutes the ultimate reference point to which all interventions and all assessments of those interventions must be related. The family's experience of the problem and their desire to make changes to remedy the situation define the *mandate* that the family gives to the therapist. The mandate from the family's perspective will define the boundary of the ongoing therapeutic work that they consent to. This mandate therefore sets a limit on the nature and extent of the interventions and approach that the therapist is 'permitted' to perform. The connection between the presenting problem and interventions is the essence of this therapeutic mandate, which then legitimises the therapeutic work.

At the completion of the initial session the therapist will summarise what has gone on with particular reference to the presenting problem and in her summary will refer to its relationship to family resilience, the difficulties they may be facing generally and their link to their social network. She will identify some themes that appear related to the solving of this difficulty and will basically outline the work that will be undertaken in order to meet the objective of the mandate:

> As we are finishing today this seems to be a good point to sum up where we've got to so far. Mr and Mrs Jones you have come along because you have been concerned about how Rob's behaviour is affecting you and him. This is

causing you difficulties not just in managing it but in how you agree to manage it. We've decided that we will talk about these issues as a family to see if we can find a way of helping with this problem and it may be that at some point we talk without Rob being in the room. We know from what we have discussed so far that it might involve talking about the different ideas that there are in your family about dealing with difficult behaviour in boys and also dealing with disagreements. Also as your parents, Mr Jones, are involved in Rob's care we might think about inviting them at some stage. We've agreed that we will meet three more times and then review how we're getting on.

Some therapists consider this agenda as a contract and introduce some formality by presenting it in a written form (Street and Downey 1996), whereas other therapists will deal with it as an informal summary at the end of the first session. Whichever tactic is employed the therapist will and should refer to it on future occasions so that the mandate and the agenda that flows from it are not lost but are available for review and for renegotiation at any time.

Part 4

THE THERAPIST'S TECHNIQUES

40

Hypothesising and formulating

Throughout the process of therapy there is a need for the therapist to construct her view of what is happening by way of a formulation or a hypothesis. This may be to lead her own questioning or to offer an alternative view to the family. For example before the first session with the Jones family the family therapist might hypothesise that Rob's behaviour seems to 'fit' between a father who expects boys to be difficult because that is how he was when he was a child and a mother who is very upset that her son is growing up and growing away from her. The therapist here may see Rob's behaviour as being 'functional', e.g. each parent contradicts the other and so they help to maintain the problem.

There are many different ways of describing the process of hypothesising. As a term it was introduced by the Milan school (Palazzoli *et al*. 1978, 1980a) of family therapy as one of their three key core techniques (the others being circularity and neutrality). Contemporary practice has tended to place less emphasis upon the process of constructing a hypothesis largely because family therapists have become cautious about ascribing causes and responsibility on family dynamics and have become more collaborative in their approach. However, even in the early descriptions of hypothesising care was taken to stress that therapists should not be 'married' to their ideas but hold them lightly and be ready to revise them in the light of therapy. So in the case of our example as more information was gained in the session the therapist developed the hypothesis that Rob is behaving the way he is because his parents are arguing all the time and he wants to distract them from their arguments by behaving badly – his behaviour is 'functional' because it prevents further family conflict. Hypothesising for the therapist therefore refers to the way she is mindfully aware of her changing ideas about the process of interaction. It has to account for different perspectives and it needs to imply a punctuation that can lead to change. If the hypothesis does include all these elements, then once again no family member should be blamed or given too much responsibility for what is happening.

For a family therapist a hypothesis is a theory about *both* how a family pattern contributed to the problem that has brought them to therapy *and* about what patterns/beliefs/behaviours might be maintaining the problem now. Some family therapists consider that both are important, whereas others emphasise the latter view (Simon 1992; Eisler 2005).

Hypotheses are important in that firstly they provide a framework for the therapist's interventions as they inform both the kinds of questions and the topics of conversation evolved by the therapist. Secondly, a hypothesis is not a secretly held 'professional' view. Rather, most hypotheses are best shared so that family members can consider how useful they are to them. Collaboration is, as we have said, the key to good therapy. For example Rob's parents might be helped to hear Rob's views about the arguments and be asked how sensible it is for them to see his behaviour as a way of stopping more arguments between themselves. Lastly, in keeping with systemic ideas, a hypothesis is really only a temporary way of viewing things that might be more or less helpful. In other words, the hypothesis does not have 'truth'. Rather, it is a temporary construction for what is happening in family life that is interchangeable with others. Even more paradoxical, the family therapist may feel that a number of hypotheses 'work' or are useful at any one time and it does not matter that they may contradict each other.

A hypothesis in systemic therapy is therefore *circular, relational* and *does not blame individuals*. So to say that 'Rob is behaving badly to stop his mother going to work' is not a systemic hypothesis. This is of course how his mother understands the behaviour. In systemic terms this hypothesis is linear: it asserts *a* (Mum goes to work) so *b* (Rob misbehaves). A more systemic hypothesis would be: 'The relationship between his mother and Rob has elements of closeness, which means that it is difficult for him to be away from her. This is possibly because his mother and father seem to argue a lot and their closeness is not obvious to Rob. By doing what he does, Rob lets everyone know he has worries about this.' Here a (a relationship) connects to b (a behaviour), which connects to c (another relationship), which connects to b (the behaviour). The pattern described in this hypothesis is therefore circular, relational and explains rather than blames. Of course, as we have noted, because circular patterns are always embedded in other circular patterns (Point 4) we have to choose to punctuate the pattern knowing that there are many other possible patterns we could comment on. This is why family therapists encourage as many hypotheses as possible and keep an open mind about the truth value of any. Thus in the Jones family an alternative hypothesis might be: 'Rob behaves as he does (a, a behaviour) because his understanding from his father is that that is how boys behave (b, a historical gender pattern) and that relationships between men and women (c, a relationship pattern) are characterised by women (in his case his Mum) criticising men.'

41

Expanding contexts

We have already explained that family therapy seeks to widen a family's understanding of any problem they come to therapy with. The first fundamental process that occurs in family therapy is that the therapist explores the problem that is described in order to expand the contexts in which it is understood. A therapist expands the family's understanding of a problem by helping them to contextualise the problem within the different 'levels of meaning' (Pearce 1994). This approach allows the therapist to accept that for many families they are 'stuck' in not knowing what to do differently because they cannot think outside of their frame of reference. In our example of the Jones family the therapist accepts their description but begins to explore with them what influences have determined how they have defined 'everything'. She will help the parents appreciate how their response is embedded in how they relate to one another. She will then move the frame of reference to find out how this response has been affected by their own family histories and how it will be affected by their ideas about gender roles in the family.

This process has been called a 'gentle conversation' in which the purpose is to unpick the levels of meaning that constrain solutions to problems. What usually emerges from this conversation is a number of themes about relationship patterns, family expectations and past history, all of which will have a bearing on the problem. Ultimately, by expanding the contexts of the problem in this way, family therapy opens up alternative responses to the problem.

Therapist: I am interested Mr Jones that you think your wife is more concerned about Rob than you. Do you mind my asking what you were like at Rob's age?

Mr Jones:	Well I guess I had the same sort of problems at home and school. Actually worse!
Therapist:	So do you think that your experience as a child makes you less worried than your wife?
Mr Jones:	I had never thought about that, but I suppose, yes. I didn't have the best childhood, my Mum and Dad were always arguing and I kind of brought myself up, and my brothers to be honest. Rob gets a lot better from us than I ever had. . .
Therapist:	Mrs Jones, do you think your husband's experience as a child affects how he thinks about Rob and what he does that you find worrying?
Mrs Jones:	Yes I think it does. Maybe he doesn't really understand what problems this might cause Rob at school.
Therapist:	Do you think making a success of school matters more to your husband than doing what his mother tells him to do?
Mrs Jones:	Yes, he wants the best for his children, he didn't get on well at school and has been unemployed for spells.

In this extract, the therapist moves between levels of context that range from gender patterns, couple relationships, historical versions of childhood and even future hopes for the children. What this does is open up the discussion. It broadens the scope for family thinking and relating. Ultimately, the intention is to help the family go away with a more complex understanding of how the problem emerged and what alternatives they might have to change it.

42

Talking about difficult subjects

Family therapy prefers to work with a multi-generational family group because it believes that stimulating the conversation between family members is an integral part of the healing process. Some family therapists describe this process as the unfolding of the 'unsaid' (Larner 2000). Sometimes what needs to be said is a family secret such as the different parentage of a child. Sometimes, it is just mundane resentments that have never been spoken about before. For instance, a wife may have stored up resentment about how she and the family have had to move to accommodate the husband's work. Sometimes, despite our belief that blame is not helpful, someone in the family has always blamed themselves for problems. Again an example might be where a father believes his daughter has anorexia because it is in his genes as his sister and mother had anorexia. In these situations, the family therapist has a role to stimulate and make safe any communication and to balance any critical communication with positive ones.

In the skills required to help family members talk about difficult subjects, the therapist must be able to manage strong feelings. This entails two specific skills. One is to 'contain' the emotions that are expressed and to constantly reframe (see Point 45) them so that other family members can hear them without being hurt. For instance, in one family the daughter was holding onto angry feelings because she felt that whilst her Mum was depressed (and misusing alcohol) she had had to care for her. She felt she had been robbed of her childhood. The therapist had to acknowledge how she felt, balance this with checking out how much her Mum could manage and also help both of them to recognise that this interaction had the potential to heal the hurt rather than consolidate it.

The second skill has various names but might be most usefully described as 'titration'. This means that the therapist has to manage the conversation and alternate the discussion if it is too difficult for any family member. This skill is essential in an interactional therapy where all family members may be present and may not be able to bear too much emotional 'heat'. The therapist might agree that 'only so much time on this subject is OK' and once that time has been reached she will change the subject. Sometimes this will require talking about everyday issues like the weather or where the family buy shoes from! At other times, if it appears to be a crucial conversation, the therapist might use other family members to lessen the intensity. In the above example, the therapist was able to ask the father how he saw this experience of his daughter's, which allowed the daughter and the mother to have a short rest from the intense feelings evoked by the issue. Alternatively, the therapist might ask 'what can I do to help us all stay focused, because I think this is important?'

43

Working with blaming interactions

Family therapists work to alleviate 'blaming' in therapy sessions for a number of reasons. Firstly, family therapists believe that no one will change if they feel criticised. This is summarised by the Milan team in the phrase that 'no one changes under a negative connotation' (Jones 1993). Secondly, blame implies that the blamer has no responsibility for solving the problem. Family therapy is a therapy that seeks to share responsibility within the system. This is a systems theory perspective: It is more helpful to understand what is maintaining the blamer's position and to enquire into how the blamer and blamed are relating rather than agree to such a polarity. Lastly, since blaming can occur in family sessions, with multiple family members present, it can be intensely painful for the blamed person to hear.

Therapeutic responses to such interactions are to use reframing (see Point 45) and to always seek the intention of the behaviour rather than concentrate on the behaviour itself. Family therapists also seek to change the way problems are talked about in therapy as soon as possible. One technique is to seek non-blaming descriptions and talk about how people behave rather than 'what they are' (Palazzoli *et al.* 1980a). Therapists will frequently move the conversation from a behavioural level towards an emotional level. This is because problems that are given as someone's 'fault' are often described on a behavioural level without thinking about what they are saying about the emotional purpose of the behaviour.

Therapist:	Have you ever asked your partner why he works so hard and is not in your terms 'there for you'?
Female partner:	It is obvious that he doesn't care for me that much.
Therapist:	Could you ask him and see what he says?

| *Female partner*: | Why do you seem to be married to your work? |
| *Male partner*: | I can't bear to be criticised by you all the time. I feel useless and no good for you, but at work I am wanted and valued. |

This concentration on the feelings behind behaviour can often quite dramatically change a process in which a family member is being blamed. It also allows the way the problem is viewed to change. In the above example it is no longer the behaviour of the male partner but the relationship that leads to his behaviour where the problem lies. The therapist seeks to open up the problem in a way that lessens blame and encourages joint responsibility taking so that solutions and collaboration can occur.

44

Constructing a family history narrative – a genogram

One very common technique of family therapists is to construct a family tree or genogram with the family in the first session (McGoldrick *et al.* 1999). A genogram is a pictorial representation of the family's history through the generations with the dates of important events included. Although this sounds like 'just' a family tree, of the sort that children draw in school, it is much more. It provides the therapist with a way of gathering historical and emotional information about the family. It also allows the family to see a pictorial representation of themselves as a whole.

To construct a genogram the therapist will need to begin with the family in front of her and then work back through history. All births, deaths and miscarriages need to be recorded together with the dates of divorces, home leavings, marriages, separations, and so on. While this information is being collected, the therapist will be noting patterns and perhaps pointing out how an event in one generation was followed within a short space of time by an event in another generation, e.g. deaths sometimes being shortly followed by a marriage, or a separation being followed by a major illness. Similarly the therapist, in a reflective way, will be investigating individuals' emotional responses to what has happened. *'How did you feel when your parents separated and which one of them was the most upset?'* There is little doubt of the impact on the family of seeing in a graphical form their family history; it is an experience that allows clients to feel embedded in the influences that have formed them. It is the process of confronting these influences that allows for the development of choice. In many instances family members will find out that even though they believed they knew their history, when they are able to look at it in a more direct written form they become aware of gaps in their knowledge. They may become aware of ways in which their history has been distorted by the perceptions of other family members. For example it might be that a family member discovers they lived longer with their grandparent or that their parents had been married for a much shorter time than they had thought previously. They can become aware of being distant and cut off from aspects of their emotional heritage. Thus completing a genogram allows for a re-establishment of important links. This lack of knowledge can be utilised to assist family members to establish helpful relationships with their extended family as well as motivating them to seek information useful to the reconstruction of how they see themselves.

The genogram is also a record of emotional closeness. The family therapist might draw jagged lines on the picture to represent conflict, or double lines to represent closeness. The therapist might notice certain inter-generational patterns of closeness, such as girls being cared for by grandmothers or fathers having to work away from the family.

Genograms that are constructed at the very beginning of therapy are primarily useful in providing a potted history of the family so that everyone is aware of who is who. Once therapy has continued for a while and the family appear to have made a good link with the therapist then the genogram can be used to relate to the more emotional aspects of the history that will become apparent.

As the genogram is being constructed questions arise from a curious therapist about how relationships operated, particularly in the way the adults were parented. When confronted with a genogram's information, asking somebody how their parents behaved and felt is likely to yield a more rounded and a fuller emotional response.

'How do you think your parents contributed to what is happening to you now?'
'What do you think your mother/father was going through when they divorced?'
'How do you think you related to your grandparents when your father left your home?'

'What made you very upset and frightened when you were a child?'

'If you were feeling sick or unhappy who would you have turned to when you were a child?'

These questions link to the way in which individuals form their attachments and construct their intimate relationships. Asking about them allows for the therapeutic process to make past events available for present experiencing. A direct experiential approach to the genogram is called sculpting (Minuchin and Fishman 1981). Here the therapist asks the family members to position themselves in the room into a spatial symbolic representation of how past relationships worked. This can then be balanced by a 'how are you now?' sculpt and a 'how would you like to be when therapy is ended?' sculpt. Other experiential techniques of use here would be using role-play to explore past events, have an adult play a child role from their family history or having photographs of past family members brought to the session.

45

Reframing and positive connotation

Family therapists are very keen to attend to language in a particular way. On the one hand they listen for phrases and language used by family members. They do this so they can create alternative descriptions of patterns, problems and persons that may be more helpful to the family. Bateson called this process the process of 'double description' (1972). What he meant was that while we have one description of a situation, there is little room to change it. Once we have more than one description (the more the better), alternatives become possible. Family therapists therefore seek to offer reframes and positive connotations as often as possible: these are respectful invitations to the family to 'see' things differently.

A reframe involves a therapist retelling or reconstructing the language used by a family about its problems. It might choose to emphasise the interactive aspects of the problem rather than its 'intrinsic nature'. It also might provide a new context that gives the problem a new meaning. A reframe is not necessarily a 'good' description. For instance, many families come with a negative description of a child, saying he or she is 'angry'. The therapist might begin to wonder if the anger is really sadness and enquire what might be going wrong in this child's life. Now, from an outside perspective, helping the family see the child as 'sad' and not 'bad' might not be greatly positive, but doing so might provide a more helpful basis for a family conversation that might lead to a better 'solution'.

Reframing was largely developed by the strategic and structural schools of family therapy (see Points 62 and 63) but positive connotation was developed by the Milan school (Palazzoli *et al.* 1978). Positive connotation is a form of reframing that differs in three fundamental ways from the family's initial ideas about the problem:

1 It considers the intent or the motivation of the behaviours that have been cast in a previously negative light and recasts them in a positive light; it positively connotes them (Palazzoli *et al.* 1980a).

2 It proposes that there is a reasonable and even possibly altruistic rationale for the problem occurring in the way it does; in other words it identifies the people involved in the problem as doing something for the benefit of others and not for just themselves.

3 It places the events, actions, thoughts and behaviour into a relational framework that emphasises their interconnectedness with other significant family events/members.

For example a family might present an adolescent who is so shy that she does not speak outside of her home and has not made any friends or developed any relationships outside of the family. Previous definitions of this problem might have included such negative connotations of the girl as being overdependent, anti-social, immature or even ill. The family may have been described as overprotective or suffocating. An intervention based on positively connoting might be presented to the family in the following words:

> I am impressed with the independence of Sheila by deciding not to become involved with other people and wishing to remain close to her family (*dependence is reframed here as independence*). After living in such a close and devoted family it seems as if she has developed the idea that if she was to grow up, make friends and spend less time at home then her parents may suffer and she wishes this not to happen. Therefore by not going out she is making sure that she will remain at home and be available to them whenever they need her (*positive connotation of the child's intention*).

Reframes and positive connotations are intended to propose new and often unexpected meanings for individual behaviour, the nature of a particular relationship and the collective interaction of a whole family system. They may allow people to change without losing face. They place solutions to the problem within the available repertoire of the family by releasing them from their currently restricted ways of considering the problem.

Throughout the therapeutic process, the therapist will be positively connoting single interactions and straightforward family attributions, such as identifying difficult behaviour as 'helpful' or suggesting that the person who does not say anything is being exceptionally 'thoughtful' about what is going on. This models a way of thinking about each other, but also introduces different perspectives in a continual way (Watzlawick *et al.* 1974; O'Brian and Bruggen 1982).

46

Assessment in family therapy

Traditionally family therapists have not given the concept of assessment as much attention as other types of therapy (Mace 1995). There are a number of reasons for this. Partly, it was argued that therapy should be brief and focused so there was little time to have a set number of assessment sessions prior to engaging in therapy. There was a further argument that if the therapist saw an issue in the first session of therapy she ought to seek to help change/deal with it there and then. In other words for family therapists assessment and treatment were blurred categories.

However, there have been a number of assessment formats created that seek to provide the therapist and the family with a thorough understanding of the way the family 'system' works so that the therapist has a clear view about what interventions should be used. The foremost of these assessment methods are the Circumplex (Olson 2000) and McMaster (Ryan *et al.* 2005) models. Each format assesses families according to a set number of dimensions. In the case of the Circumplex model, these are the family's adaptability and cohesion. In the case of the McMaster format it is communication, problem solving, affective responsiveness and behaviour control. The aim in each model is to ascertain upon which dimension most treatment is required. Thus in the Circumplex model, if a family were 'enmeshed' (overly emotionally cohesive) the therapist would seek to help them become more individuated (less close). In the McMaster framework, if a family rated low on problem solving, the therapist would help them learn new and more adaptable problem-solving skills.

However, in most family therapy practice assessment is a much less formal and discrete entity than implied by these formal models (Lieberman 1995). Most family therapists 'assess' while at the same time intervening. They are usually asking the following questions:

- How does this family work? In this question, the therapist will be finding out about family life, aspects of closeness/ conflicts. Typically, as mentioned earlier, the therapist will use a family genogram to gather some of this information.
- How does the problem that has brought the family to therapy relate to the way the family is? Here the therapist will be helping the family connect the way they are as a family with the way the problem is manifested. Typically, this will entail the use of circular questions, which will map the problem and its relationship to family relationships. In some cases, this question can be divided into two complementary questions: How has the family affected the problem (caused and maintained)?/How has the problem affected the family (constrained relationships)?
- What relationship changes are needed in order to improve the problem? Again this may include changes in understandings, in communication or in behaviour.
- What resources does the family have to help make these changes happen? This is a crucial question. Having this in mind avoids the assumption that the family are somehow incapable or incompetent (family therapists prefer to avoid the word 'dysfunction'). One of the insights of family therapy is that families have already often managed quite difficult transitions and so may only need small encouragements to solve problems.

It is, of course, possible that some families do not have the resources to make the changes needed to resolve problems. This conclusion, though unpalatable, is certainly possible when family therapists are asked to help families where child abuse issues have occurred (see Point 91). It is also important to accept that family therapy is not a 'cure all' therapy. Clearly at times family therapy will enable families to cope with extreme difficulties rather than resolve them. For instance, where a family member has a terminal illness, family therapy cannot 'cure' the problem but it can help family members talk about and cope better within the situation (Fredman 1997).

47

Building motivation to change

From a systems perspective, motivation is not a personality trait or something that is an intrinsic given. The desire for change and the willingness to embark on working with change are produced by the context in which the family operates and particularly by the therapeutic context that the therapist creates. Motivation is therefore contextual (Steinglas 2009). Building motivation is an important and essential task during the early discussions about the problem. As we have mentioned, many families come to therapy to assert that 'if only x would change life would be good' or 'if only x would stop interfering we would be OK as a family'. In such cases, the family therapist helps the family become aware that these are unlikely to be adequate solutions to the problem in question, therefore interest and involvement are built up by interrogating such beliefs with curiosity.

Father: If only he would learn to stop misbehaving and do what his mother wants, life for all of us would be much better.

Therapist: If that happened do you think other problems would emerge?

The family therapist will always seek to place motivation in relation to other family members and to explore with the family the different attitudes and orientations to the problem.

Therapist: Who is most keen to get this problem sorted?
Father: I am.
Therapist: That is interesting; do you have a theory about why you care more about solving this than your wife?

By highlighting such variations in motivation, the therapist seeks to increase what might be called the *motivation of the system.* This would also apply to the person who is labelled as the 'problem': *'Joe, I am wondering if you have any ideas about why your Dad is so keen to solve this problem?'* By talking with the 'problem carrier' (or 'designated patient') the family therapist is both avoiding blaming that person and inviting him into a conversation not about 'the problem' but about 'people wanting to solve the problem'. In initiating this conversation, the desire to be involved and to be a part of the solution increase.

This approach can also be combined with the more traditional motivational interviewing approach (Miller and Rollnick 2002) in which the therapist helps family members work out what the positives and negatives are to changing the problem presented. Again, however, the family therapist does this interactionally and in the room rather than with an individual only. For example the therapist might ask a parent what were the advantages of their child maintaining its difficulty (this might be called a paradoxical intervention by the Milan School). This would allow all family members to hear what might be going on that stops change occurring.

Therapist:	What do you think Jane gets out of staying anorexic?
Mother:	I think she thinks she becomes special to us.
Therapist:	Do you think that matters to other family members?
Mother:	Now you ask . . . yes. I have always been frightened about her growing up and going out with boys and stuff.
Therapist:	Does anyone else share this worry?
Mother:	Yes my mother always wanted me to stay and look after her after my Dad died . . .

Also in thinking 'outside' of the system, the family therapist may enquire of family members what other professionals/friends/ work colleagues might think about any proposed changes. Of course, ultimately these interventions may fail to elicit any motivation. This would usually mean that the family are not 'customers' but 'complainants', by which we mean they have been sent for therapy and have no intrinsic wish for therapy at all (see

Point 34). A strategic approach to this situation would be to spend time thinking with the family about how they might 'appease' the referring agent without doing any therapy. This tack is often used when families are made to attend therapy within a statutory agency's procedures, usually because abuse is considered to have occurred.

Because the primary language of family therapy is that of relationships and connections between people, motivation is also built up in the early sessions of therapy by eliciting statements of responsibility: '*When your wife says that she doesn't think you love her, what does that make you think?*' In constantly coming back to what each family member does or thinks about what other members say, family therapists engage each family member in the conversation, which encourages interest, involvement and engagement: '*What do you do when she says this? What do you think you could do to help him understand a bit better?*' The language that is used always attempts to place the family members in a set of intentional interactions in which ultimately they have a choice about what it is they do: '*So when you say that, what do you hope it will achieve?*'

48

Encounter moments and process change

In the therapeutic process that occurs between family members and the therapist there are particular types of person-to-person encounter that have an effect on how the process continues. Sometimes it seems as if these moments of encounter constitute change itself. These encounters can be seen in three dimensions:

1   Initially the most charged encounter or interaction takes place between family members as they hear each other's statements and feelings, often for the first time. The therapist has the task of catalysing the 'opening up process', which allows for the creation of new information and hence different interactions between family members. As the process unfolds a family come to trust the therapist's ability to contain the difficult emotions and thoughts that arise and hence this allows for the intensity of the family confrontation to deepen and solutions to develop.

2   The second area of encounter is between each family member and the therapist as the therapist. In demonstrating her compassion, empathy and integrity she provides a model for relating that acts as a visible alternative to the family. This encounter develops in different ways for different individuals depending on their attitude, their personality, their age, their gender and their family roles. Ideally, this leads to the family appreciating the variety of moulds of relationship that are possible within the composition of the family. These encounters lead to the development of a culture of caring within the family that is necessary for it to go on and function effectively.

3   The final area of encounter is more difficult to describe and has been called that of 'existential moments' between the therapist and individual family members (see interview with Carl Whitaker in Haley and Hoffman 1967). It is built upon

the increasing personal involvement of each family member with the therapist in the therapy process. It might first be experienced when the therapist's intuition, honesty and openness radically connect with a family member. Sometimes the experience for the family member is that they have been 'understood' in a meaningful way. This might have been preceded by a discussion that released heartfelt deep emotions, not only in the client but also in the therapist. There may be a feeling of 'transcending' the limited 'self' that the family member has adopted with a vision of new kinds of self that are available to enact. During these encounters, the rest of the family witness and are then encouraged to comment on how they understood either the process that caused this 'self to self' meeting or the consequences of it. Sometimes these events revolve around moments where forgiveness (Walrond-Skynner 1998) is talked about, or when individuals honestly talk about what they think they have done 'wrong'.

This emphasis on 'moments' of change needs to be balanced by a recognition that sometimes it is the process of the therapy that contributes to change. Sometimes this process is harder to notice: the gentle unfolding of family expectations, the careful balancing of perceptions, the constant search for understanding, the curious attention to the way relationships are constructed in the therapy room itself (between family and therapist). In these ways of describing the family therapy process, there is less concentration upon the 'techniques' and the 'interventions' and more upon the gradual unfurling. Here family therapy begins to sound more like psychodynamic psychotherapy rather than the radical alternative to it that its early pioneers proposed (Pocock 2006).

Part 5

DEVELOPING INTERVENTIONS

49

Circular questions

We have already indicated that the use of questions is central to family therapy practice. Indeed family therapists have given to psychotherapeutic practice a greater appreciation of the value of a well crafted question than any other gift (O'Brian and Bruggen 1982; Penn 1982; Brown 1997). Before describing the use of questions in family therapy however, we should establish the driving purpose of those questions. This is because a family interview should not consist of question after question in an endless, unconnected stream. Such a process would surely alienate even the most conscientious family. Rather, the questions that the therapist asks are directed by two concerns. The first is that they follow a 'theme', e.g. an issue that has relevance to the concern that has brought the family. Traditionally, questions are formulated around the hypotheses created by the therapist, team and family, but as therapy proceeds relevant family themes will emerge that may have only a tangential relationship to the original hypotheses. However the theme emerges, it should be held in mind by the therapist who gradually and purposefully uses questions to widen the scope and relational patterns connected to it. This requires a degree of persistence by the therapist: Essentially if the theme is useful then more questions are better to help achieve a difference of view. Secondly, sometimes the therapist will hear a phrase or a 'symbolic' behaviour, which again should be held in mind and returned to with a series of questions. Examples of such 'symbols' might be repeated patterns of behaviour, certain important family rituals and sometimes just repeated phrases.

It was the Milan school of family therapy (Palazzoli *et al.* 1980a) that first called the primary questions used by family therapists 'circular'. Since then there have been many embellishments on the theme (e.g. Penn 1982). Tomm (1988) has constructed the most helpful way of categorising circular questions, which we will use here.

Essentially, a circular question is *circular* because it seeks to connect what one family member does, thinks or wants with another family member: *'When your wife says that, what do you think Mr Jones?'* At a very basic level, the circular question is an intervention that is encouraging family members to connect themselves with each other. In terms of the problem that a family has come to therapy with, circular questions are asked in order to achieve a number of purposes:

- They connect the problem with behaviours, meanings or emotions between family members: *'Have you noticed that Rob behaves worse or better when you are feeling sad Mrs Jones?. . . . Have you noticed something similar when you are in more pain Mr Jones?'*
- They connect current problems with past problems: *'Did you think your husband was more or less like Rob when he was his age, Mrs Jones?'*
- They structure a 'witnessing' process for family members such that each family member may learn how they are experienced/perceived by other family members: *'When your husband says you are making too much of a fuss, does that make you think he understands you well or not so well Mrs Jones?'*
- They encourage 'inner reflection' on patterns, meanings and behaviours: *'How would you feel Mr Jones, if your wife was sure that your feelings were wrong?'*

Tomm (1988) suggests that circular questions can be learnt as a technique more fully if they are divided into certain categories outlined by the *intention* of the therapist. Thus if the therapist is asking a question to help a family member learn something, the question may have a *strategic* intent. Thus the circular question asked of Mr Jones above was intended to help Mr Jones see things from the perspective of his wife. Alternatively, however, some questions are designed to encourage the family member to find their own answer. These kinds of questions are *reflexive* because they are designed to help the family member reflect upon themselves in some way: '*Rob tell me, do you find that the way your Dad thinks about how you behave is more helpful to you than your Mum's way of thinking?*'

50

Using questions to clarify and expand

Throughout all sessions the therapist will be attempting, for the family's benefit, to clarify the process of any particular sequence of events and the meaning put on those events by the participants. Families become quite fixed in how they view a problem and the events that surround it: They assume that the friendly observer will see events in exactly the same way as he or she does. Each will also assume that the words they use to describe the event will instantly convey an exact impression of what occurred. The therapist's task is to very gently confront these assumptions by asking questions. In this process the family can become aware of new elements in what was previously considered to be familiar. Clarifying the description of individuals and expanding on the meaning that they ascribe to those descriptions is therefore a basic intervention that occurs throughout the therapy. This is done initially by 'slowing down time' and then making a link to another level of meaning so that the individual and family begin to experience a degree of flexibility in their thinking. One process by which this is done is to introduce into the question another time frame.

We can think of four different types of time frames in families: (a) seconds to hours, (b) days to a week, (c) several weeks to a year and (d) those issues that span at least one generation. Time frames (a) and (b) usually include short passages of interaction, whereas when time frames of up to one year (c) are talked about this usually involves someone discussing how their relationship seems to work. Life scripts and family myths are usually invoked when the time frame covers more than one generation (d). What invariably happens in families is that the person who is describing the interaction will focus just on one time frame and the therapist can then use that time frame but use *questions that introduce another time frame*, and by this process other types of meaning are introduced into the discussion.

Mr Harris is talking about the discussion that he had with his wife about his son's behaviour.

Mr Harris: She said she was not bothered but she was very angry about it.

Therapist: So she was saying she wasn't interested but underneath she seemed to be angry. Is that something that happens between you very often or is it only about this issue?

Mr Harris: Yes she does that a lot and it does affect how we get on.

Therapist: And is that similar or different to anybody else you know in your family?

Mr Harris: Well I suppose it reminds me of how my mother and father deal with things and I end up thinking oh no not again.

Another effective means of clarifying and expanding is to ask questions of the family about the things that they actually observed. When the family realise that the therapist is attempting to frame a composite view of the events in a whole then they readily come to answer questions from the observer's perspective. Before one can take any new action in any social setting one needs to be able to 'observe' that social setting. *Observer perspective questions* serve in helping family members become aware of the situation as it is seen by each person and in doing this each individual is given the opportunity of clarifying exactly what happens for everyone else. Each person therefore can expand their vision of what is taking place.

Therapist: Peter, your father said that when he was talking with your mother about what you were doing she said she wasn't bothered but she seemed to be very angry about it. Is that what you saw?

Peter: Well when Dad talks about what I do he becomes very angry and it's difficult to have any kind of conversation with him about it. I think that's why Mum says she is not

	bothered so that she can get out of the way of what might become an argument.
Therapist:	Sue is that how you see what happens?
Sue (sister):	Well I'm not usually there; these arguments about Peter always seem to take place when I'm out of the way.
Therapist:	But from what you 'see' or 'don't see' is Peter usually there when your mother and father are trying to have this discussion.
Sue:	Yes I think he is usually there.

The therapist is also keen to ask questions that clarify distinctions, so in the above dialogue some other clarifying questions would be: *'What does "not bothered" mean?'* *'How do you know when Mother is "not bothered"?'* *'What does angry mean?'* *'Is mother angry in a different way to father?'* As always, the curious stance provokes many different questions.

51

Using questions to open communication

Family members who say 'the trouble with us is that we do not communicate' certainly do not have an interactive perspective. Families that face a problem in communicating need to appreciate that it is not the lack of communication but the nature of their communication that is not helpful in finding a solution to their problem. It is likely that the communication they embark on is repetitive and hence it will not be generating new information. The therapist therefore, in attempting to open communication, should see her activity as ensuring that the family are aware of how they communicate and then helping that communication develop towards the problem at hand. The most important way to do this in the initial phases of therapy is to focus on the individuals so that each person can become aware of their own activity in relation to the activity of others. By encouraging this kind of communication, the therapist helps each family member become better able at informing others about their own feelings and thoughts. This process is simply done by asking people how they were thinking and feeling at a particular time, followed by asking them how they believed other family members were thinking and feeling at the same time. Then, by asking similar questions of the other members present in a way that has a natural conversational flow about it, the therapist acts as a channel aiming to help family members 'hear' the views of everyone.

Therapist: Mrs Harris, when you tell your husband that you're not bothered about something that you might be angry about, what is going through your mind?

Mrs Harris: I'm thinking that I'm going to get it wrong, that if I say anything I will be told that I don't understand it.

Therapist:	What do you think your husband thinks?
Mrs Harris:	I don't know really, he's just doing things his way.
Therapist:	And what about your son, what do you think is going on for him?
Mrs Harris:	I think he's making sure that we don't argue too much, that he's watching over me somehow to make sure I don't get shouted at as well.
Therapist:	Is that what is happening for you Peter?

Problems can arise with this type of questioning if there is too much focus on a specific individual and there is no sharing out of information about the event from the perspective of others. When one individual provides too much information from his or her own perspective the therapist needs to clarify whether this is the same information that is communicated at home and in so doing the perspective of others will be brought into the discussion.

These questions begin the communicational process because by asking each individual to comment on 'myself as I see me', then onto 'other individuals as I see them', the therapist can easily manoeuvre the family members into talking about 'me as others see me'. This establishes the process of speaking, active listening and reflection on what has been heard. The next layer involves 'my relationship with person A as it is seen by person B'. Some have described this style of questioning as almost socially rude and as 'gossiping in the presence of others' (Palazzoli 1974). It sometimes evokes the answer 'I don't know, why don't you ask him!'. But in our example: *'Peter, what are you thinking when your mother and father have that discussion about you?'* Here Mr Harris has the opportunity to hear about his relationship with his wife as it is seen by Peter, and Mrs Harris has a similar opportunity. This is known as *triadic questioning* as it involves a third person commenting on how the others behave.

52

Using questions to break repetitive patterns

Families with problems repeat the same interaction over and over. It is as if they have a set dance and each family will 'dance their dance' if given the opportunity to do so. For each problem they will have developed, over time, a particular way of dealing with each other. Each will have their own assigned roles and each will play it to the full whenever the sequence is started. When these patterns occur within sessions they can result in family members feeling that the whole process is hopeless and hence when they occur repeatedly they can seriously undermine the therapy. In essence the therapist's task is to stop the repetitive process and then analyse what happens in terms of interactions and associated feelings/thoughts. The therapist should then explore some alternative ways of considering that particular interactive event.

Families need to experience a situation in which the therapist has been able to tolerate, contain and confront them as they dance their dance. This is achieved by being able to stop the interaction directly, not in a commanding manner but in a way that insists a particular question be answered at that time. The therapist intervenes by moving the family away from the repetitive interaction into a discussion about the interaction. The therapist in effect takes charge of the problematic interaction by inviting family members to talk about it. The therapist will be using *process interrupting questions* to help structure the situation and contain what is occurring.

Peter: But Mum have you thought why we argue. It's you, you just won't stand up to him. Every time it's the same. You need to do something about it. Why do you let it go on for so long? I just don't understand how you put up with so much.

151

Therapist:	(*Extends his hand to Peter with a slowdown motion and looks at Mrs Harris*) Mrs Harris, Peter seems angry at this moment, does this happen at home?
Mrs Harris:	Yes I suppose it does.
Therapist:	And just as I saw here, do you just remain quiet?

The therapist here has been able to stop the son's anger towards his mother escalating and the family now need to experience this repetitive pattern in a different way. The therapist begins by seeking a description of the pattern:

Therapist:	Peter, what happened there when you got angry?
Peter:	Well it's Mum, she just won't stand up for herself.
Therapist:	Yes I appreciate you believe your mother doesn't stand up for herself. What I want to know is how you saw what just happened, you know, from your perspective what took place just now?
Peter:	Well Mum seemed to be blaming us for arguing and I wanted to tell her I thought she could do things different.
Therapist:	What did you notice your mother do?
Peter:	She just becomes quiet.
Therapist:	And your sister?
Peter:	She looked fed up and she withdrew.
Therapist:	So you were arguing and you felt blamed, you started shouting at your Mum and she becomes quiet and she and your sister withdraw. Is that what everyone saw?

Questions that explore the exact opposite in meaning and context help move a family away from a destructive pattern that occurred. So with our dialogue in which the issue seems to be about Mrs Harris not standing up for herself, a question that might be asked would be: '*Mr Harris, are there occasions on which you feel your wife does not withdraw and seems to stand up for herself?'*

Throughout the example we see that one of the aspects of the therapist's contribution is that she labels and confronts intentions and feelings in this unhelpful process. She deals directly with what is happening despite its rawness for the individuals and it is this willingness to contain the difficulty that helps create a safe space in the therapy.

53

Using questions to link time – the past and present

Families with problems are often so focused on the present difficulties or on past history that they function as if there is no future. Tomorrow is experienced as just a piece of today. Such an orientation provides a paucity of problem-solving strategies, as no alternative ways of behaviour are considered (Boscolo and Bertrando 1993). The therapist therefore has to investigate the way the family considers its present-day behaviour in terms of the past or future. This is not only done to bring to awareness the domination of another time over the present, but it is also done to elaborate on past or future events that the family have not considered in the search of solutions. Each family will have some hidden or neglected strengths in their history and similarly a more reflexive, hopeful view of the future can create new opportunities.

In terms of her investigation into the family's time continuum, the therapist should bear in mind that each family, broadly speaking, will categorise past and future time for themselves into three past periods and two future periods. We will begin with a consideration of past time:

1   *Historical time*. This is the time that in an intact family is before the adult couple came together and, going back, includes those relationships observed as a child and those adult relationships of family members that have ceased. The importance of this time is that it may well contain patterns of relating that dominate the present and potentially could offer alternatives to present-day relating. Family members need to be helped in feeling linked to the positive but psychologically separated from the negative elements of their family's history.

2   *'Before' time*. Families can readily refer to a time before the problem emerged. This may be the time before a major illness, before the husband had an affair or before a particular developmental stage was reached. The therapeutic task

is to realistically appraise family functioning at this 'before time' in order to prevent the scapegoating of the person who 'has' the identified problem, as well as utilising past useful family interactions that may have withered away. Here, by questioning, the therapist will be attempting to retrieve this time so that its beneficial qualities may be applied to the present.

3   *'Last week'*. This is the period of time just prior to the session. Frequently, however, the whole history of the problem may seem to be defined solely in terms of last week. Each family will need to review last week in realistic terms so that the idea of the problem can be seen as having a change element through time, for if changing past time can be demonstrated then changing future time is also likely.

Therapist:	Mrs Davies I know you feel that your husband is not that interested in your feelings. Has there been a time when he was bothered?
Mrs Davies:	Well yes, when we were first married and then when the children were much younger, everything was okay then.
Therapist:	It was easier for him and you then at the beginning of your marriage?
Mrs Davies:	Yes it was.
Therapist:	And was it like the kind of bothering you were used to when you were a child?
Mrs Davies:	Yes, it seemed to be something that I was used to and it just seemed to carry on in the same way.
Therapist:	So when did it seem as if your husband stopped being bothered?
Mrs Davies:	Perhaps gradually. The children got older. I went back to work, Peter went away to university and things became different?
Therapist:	So he changed over that time? When I ask him do you think he will say that you have changed over that time too?

Mrs Davies: I'm sure he will say I've changed (*husband nods*). But I still feel the same. I'm not sure in what way I've changed.

Therapist: So if you're not sure and I ask you to compare how you were, shall we say, last week with how you were when you first got married, how do you think that was different?

54

Using questions to link time – the future and present

Families who are so fearful of things in the future live their present life seemingly in an endless task of preventing future events from occurring. They continue as if there is no natural change process as development occurs. As the future seems to contain negatives, the possibility of doing something different is just not considered. Such is the overfocus on trying to hold things the same, that the range of present-day behaviour is severely hampered and the development of a range of behaviour that could extend into the future is just not seen as being possible. The therapist should therefore ask questions about future time, specifically linking it to present events as well as things that have happened in the past. In the way in which families conceive of time there are two future time dimensions:

1   *Next week.* Nearly all families will see next week as being potentially different from last week. Once a realistic description of what transpired last week has occurred, then it becomes useful to juxtapose that with questions about what may happen next week. Again, if in the process of reflexive questioning the family acquires a sense of a problem being variable through time, then the straightforward question *'what will you do next week?'* spontaneously introduces the notion of choice within a context that may change. One particular category of questioning that is important about 'next week' is that which deals with the expectations that individuals may have about events following what transpires in the therapy session itself. For example, if two people have argued in the session or a family member has said something for the first time, the question would be *'since that happened here today, what do you think will happen about it when you go home or in the next day or two?'*

159

Here the therapist is clearly making links between the present and the immediate future so that family members can communicate openly about the events as well as point out the importance of the process of change between sessions.

2 *The 'future'.* Thoughts about the future can, to a considerable extent, determine present behaviour. Whether the future inappropriately dominates current action or whether the family do not consider it at all, the therapist does need to ensure that the distant future is seen as having a role in the present. Even though asking about future eventualities may not produce much in the verbal output of family members, this certainly is a category of question that family members take home with them and work out in their own way. First the therapist needs to confront the negative view of the future in terms of asking about the potential outcome if the problem remains: *'If your son and husband continued to argue, what do you think will happen?'* This can then be extended into a *catastrophic expectation question*: *'If you don't manage to do something about this difficulty, what is the very worst thing that could happen?'* Another type of questioning concerns the exploration of hypothetical possibilities. Here the therapist constructs a scenario that may or may not have some possibility of occurring and questions family members about how such an event would unfold. *'Mrs Davies, supposing you and your daughter were out when your son called. How do you think he and his father would get on then?'* The type of future-orientated question that leads naturally into identifying problem-solving strategies is one that asks about future goals. *'What plans do you have for dealing with the situation next time it arises?'* Future-orientated questions are also necessary as they clearly imply that the future belongs to the family. It is their responsibility, with the therapist playing no role.

Therapist: Mr Davies, as you have heard, your wife has said that she thinks that you are not that bothered about her feelings. I could ask you what you want to do about that now in the room with us all here but I suppose the most important question is how are you going to respond to that when you go home?

Mr Davies: I'm obviously upset that she thinks that and I would like to talk to her about what she thinks should happen so that it doesn't seem like that. It's because I am bothered about how she feels.

Therapist: And do you think yourself that something needs to change so that in the future, when the children have left home and you two are together on your own again, things might be the same as they were initially?

55

Asking questions to place behaviour in a normative context

All families construct ideologies to explain certain events and experiences (see Point 31). With repeating difficulties these ideologies come to dominate how family members respond to particular behaviours. However, sometimes a piece of behaviour might be within the normal limits that one would expect of a person of that developmental stage in that context, but the family has failed to see it in this way. Families vary in the extent to which they believe themselves to be different from others and it is a common occurrence for individuals and families to feel that they are abnormal when they encounter a common difficulty. As this occurs frequently, there are typical 'myths' that feed the idiosyncratic ideas that families have about particular problems.

- If you're caring for a chronically ill or handicapped person you should do this willingly and happily and not experience any difficult emotions.
- Whenever someone such as a child behaves in a difficult manner, there is always a reason for this, which is to do with the extent to which they wish to get at somebody.
- All children should behave at all times and if they do not they should respond to reasoned arguments.
- Negative feelings in one family member are always caused by another family member.

Such notions interfere with the family's problem-solving ability and normative behaviour can therefore come to be seen as being a problem. Families therefore need help in understanding what behaviour can reasonably be expected to occur in a particular context. In such circumstances the therapist's task is, by her questioning, to invite the family into a more normative frame and towards more appropriate expectations. The therapist does not wish to imply to the family that they are 'getting it wrong', rather, what is required is the gentle clarification of their view of the problem and then the asking of questions that invite family members to consider a normative comparison. Such questions may be:

'How much do you think this is typical of a person with that chronic illness?'
'To what extent do you think his behaviour is the same as other 10-year-olds?'
'How much do you think she behaves like that because she is in a wheelchair or is it because she's an average 16-year-old?'
'What do you think is the usual emotional reaction when a man loses his job?'
'How typical do you think your son's behaviour is in coming home so late in the evening?'

In effect the therapist is inviting the family to consider by how much they are meeting normal events and this is utilised in their desire to be the same as other people. It may be that following the client's answers the therapist introduces some of his own professional or even personal experience. This may be a way in which the behaviour is placed in a normative context.

Sometimes the therapist uses such questions to highlight for the family that there is something happening that is *not* normative. For instance, a therapist might say: '*If a friendly neighbour of yours was to tell me about your family what do you think she or he would say?*' This question would encourage family members to see the difference between themselves and a 'normative' idea of family life.

56

Investigating problem-solving solutions

In moving towards identifying strategies that will aid in the solving of the problem brought by the family, the therapist should link the family's process of making changes in the past with the change process that hopefully is to come. Initially this is done by finding out the strategies that family members have attempted in the past. There are several reasons for doing this:

1 The family's usual mechanism of solving problems needs to be understood by all.
2 Family members need to feel that they have embarked on some problem-solving earlier and that this had good elements as well as encountering difficulties.
3 The therapeutic system needs to identify those factors that the family see as blocking solutions.
4 The therapist needs to have a good appreciation of what failed and why, so that she does not go on and simply make suggestions that merely repeat the family's history.

The means of identifying previous solutions is simply to ask: *'What have you attempted in the past to sort out this problem?'*

> *Therapist:* Mrs Davies, have you done anything in the past to stop Peter from arguing with his father?
>
> *Mrs Davies:* At the beginning I used to ask them not to do it again politely after it was over.
>
> *Therapist:* Did you ask them both together or did you talk to them separately?
>
> *Mrs Davies:* Separately. I would do it very quietly to each of them.

Therapist: So after it was over you'd find some time to say something to both of them individually about it?

The next question concerns the solutions that individuals have considered but have not attempted. Usually these types of solutions are things that people have thought privately but have not shared with others.

Therapist: Sue have you thought to yourself of any way you might help your father and Peter stop arguing?

Sue: Not really, I try to stay out of Peter's way about this. I'm not sure how to say anything to my father.

Therapist: So for you the only solution is not to get involved with either of them?

Should any individual indicate that they have thought of a solution that has not been tried, it is important to clarify the reasons why not and to look at the advantages and disadvantages of that solution.

Therapist: Mr Davies, you did say that you had thought about going to see Peter in his own flat? How is it that you've not done that?

Mr Davies: I'm not sure if I'd know what to say. It is difficult for us to have an ordinary conversation.

Therapist: Mrs Davies, do you think that there might be something that would work if your husband went to see Peter on his own ground?

This concentration on what has been tried to solve the problem is an intervention that has roots in both the MRI school of family therapy (Watzlawick *et al.* 1974; Fisch 2004) and also reflects ideas with solution-focused therapy (de Shazer 1988).

57

Making suggestions within questions

Nearly all families require some help in framing possible solutions and the therapist may find it necessary to find ways of making suggestions to them. A strategy for offering a solution without making it seem too much like a direct suggestion is the *embedded suggestion question*. Here the therapist aims to point the family in a direction that may prove useful and does this by asking a variant of the 'what if' question; such questions can be asked about actions, beliefs or feelings.

Therapist:	Obviously there are a lot of difficult feelings behind this situation but what do you think would happen if you suggested to Peter that he limited the amount of time he came and visited you?
Mrs Davies:	I haven't thought about that. (*To Peter*) What would you think?
Peter:	I don't know but it could be difficult for me.
Sue:	He means he would have to do his own washing.
Therapist:	Well a lot of things may need to be negotiated about that.

The tone of the therapist's voice and the choice of particular words make a considerable difference to the degree to which the suggestion is embedded and the likelihood that it is seen as just a question and not an instruction. The tone of the question therefore needs to be definite enough to have family members hold it within their minds at least for a while, but not too definite so that the question ceases to be a question. If asked well these questions can be very powerful, in that the family is invited to internally construct an image of a different interactive sequence for themselves.

The value of such questions is also that they allow the therapist and the family to experiment, to try out different ways of thinking and feeling and relating. To ensure this happens the therapist needs to ensure that everybody's views about the possible events are included: '*Mr Davies what would it be like for you if your son did not come around so often?*' Similarly it is important to ask questions that encourage interpersonal perception about the event. '*Sue, how do you think your mother will feel if Peter does not come around so much?*' The purpose of this is to bring into the open how one individual perceives the actions, beliefs and feelings of another person within the confines of the change. Sometimes the therapist will talk about such a change being an experiment: '*Let's say you tried this out as an experiment, say for a few days; who would find it hardest?*'

Such embedded suggestion questions were first described by Milton Erickson in his hypnotic techniques (Erickson *et al.* 1976; Erickson and Rossi 1981). Family therapists have probably adopted these questions because they believe that normal 'advice' will have failed to help most of the families they see. Moreover, like Erickson, they largely believe that advice is 'resisted' by most people (Haley 1976).

58

Enactment

At times the therapist will need to gain access to the usual interactive pattern in the family rather than learning about it only from their descriptions. Although a questioning stance does provide a considerable amount of information it often does not allow for that information to be emotionally condensed in a way that has meaning within 'real' time. A therapeutically helpful way of actually watching family interaction is to request members of the family to enact a particular interactional event within the session (Minuchin and Fishman 1981). This usually takes the form of a discussion between two people on a theme that is relevant to the issues being discussed in therapy or on a constructed task provided by the therapist. This is called *enactment*. The purposes of the enactment are:

- To enable the therapist to see how the members interact rather than hear them describe how they believe they interact.
- To push the interactions beyond their usual threshold in order to test out how flexible the family system actually is.
- To enable family members to try out different types of interaction within the safe environment of therapy.

It is useful to think of the process of enactment as occurring in three phases. In the first phase the therapist is observing the family whilst interacting with them and then becomes aware of spontaneously repeating sequences that indicate particular family characteristics. Such sequences may be: who talks to whom, who interrupts who, how the parents talk to each other and then to the children, etc. In the second phase, the family or parts of the family are requested to enact a sequence around a particular issue, which allows the therapist to become more of an observer. In the final stage, the therapist is more active and may slow down the interaction sequence; she may ask questions about it, try to involve different combinations of family members or even suggest particular things that people could do, to see what the effect is. The aim of the final stage is to allow the family to experience a new way of interacting.

Using enactments can be very useful in actively engaging family members in therapy, especially if there is a wide range of ages. If the therapist has become rather 'stuck' (see Point 82) and the therapy has a repetitive pattern to it, enactment is a very useful strategy for helping the therapist step outside that process. Typical enactments may involve:

- Having parents of adolescent children discuss how they are going to deal with the children's behaviour while the children simply look on.
- Having parents and children 'switch' roles and pretend to be each other.
- Encouraging a typical argument to happen and helping family members to resolve it differently.

It is also quite common for families to engage in spontaneous enactments.

Mother: Do you think I undermine you when it comes to the children?

Father: Yes I do, just the other day you did it when I said he couldn't go out.

Mother: Oh, I don't notice that I do it, what should I do instead?

Father: Maybe we could talk about why I make some decisions and decide if you agree before we say anything to the children.

Here the therapist might help these parents to establish the new pattern by getting them to role-play this situation and then to do this talking.

59

Homework tasks

Homework tasks in family therapy are not the same as assignments given in behavioural therapy (Haley 1976). Although some family tasks may resemble and indeed be inspired by a behavioural frame, they are dealt with differently because in family therapy even though the therapist is interested in the outcome of a task more importantly she is interested in the 'task as information' to the therapeutic system. Whether the task 'succeeds' or 'fails' it will still provide important information about family interaction and hence maintain the momentum of therapy. Setting tasks or homework clearly places responsibility for problem-solving within the client system. The therapist should be very clear in what she expects to happen and she should ensure that each person has a role within the task. If there are 'non-active' family members then they should be instructed to carefully observe the behaviour of the active ones.

The actual nature of the task will be suggested by the themes that are being followed in the therapy session. In our example of the Davies family an obvious task will be having Mr Davies visit his son and report back to his wife on how he felt about it and have Sue just observe her parents after the visit has happened. All tasks will obviously involve family members doing something together, letting each other know what it is they have done and how they considered it has gone.

There are a variety of outcomes from the task that need to be followed up within the following session:

- *A straightforward successful solution.* Everything goes well and everybody agrees it was a very positive outcome. So Mr Davies does visit his son, chats to his wife about it and his daughter sees that everyone is happy. Such events do occur. Often talking to a therapist is enough to mobilise the resources of the family to follow through with the simplest solution that they might not have been able to have undertaken themselves. However, the therapist is well advised not to seek a quick solution in the first homework task as families may need several attempts to provide new information and new interactions for themselves before new patterns can become established.

- *A new opportunity*. Different or novel interaction can occur as a consequence of the task and family members will have their own experience of it such that an exploration and clarification by the therapist may provide considerably more 'newness' than was originally created by the task performance.
- *A different task*. Sometimes families undertake a different task to the one that the therapist provided for them and the outcome provides a means of understanding the 'distortion of communication' process. The therapist needs to openly compare what he had anticipated happening with what did happen and thereby identify one of the family's typical patterns of communication that is likely to have led to the 'different' task. So perhaps, in our example, Mr and Mrs Davies went together to visit their son because that was what they thought they were being asked to do.
- *Testing commitment*. A task can also provide an opportunity to assess how family members view their involvement in therapy. Even though all the families members agree that a task is a useful thing, unfortunately at the next session the task does not seem to have been undertaken by some family members. For example, Mr Davies visits his son and his son is not at home. When such an event occurs the therapist should carefully return to the individual's expectation of therapy and commitment to it.

When families are assigned homework tasks it is very important that such tasks are monitored very early on in the following session. To ignore the task and the family's relationship with it, is to imply that it was not important.

60

Working with family scripts

As a therapist is investigating a family history, especially in relation to repeating patterns or the way particular developmental events are dealt with, it is highly likely that family scripts and family myths will become readily apparent (see Points 6 and 7). *Family scripts* (Byng-Hall 1995) are family belief systems based on scenarios within the family of origin that create expectations about general rules, roles and routines that will be undertaken within the current family.

> 'Is there a particular way in which the oldest son is expected to behave in your family?'
> 'Do you think that in your family history there is a particular attitude towards single unmarried women?'

Family myths (Bagarozzi and Anderson 1989) are active stories that can be repeated by family members, usually based on a distorted account of historical events within the family of origin. These stories lay a foundation for how particular events and particular types of people will be dealt with. Family myths stipulate that particular ways of behaving should occur or should not appear when particular situations are confronted.

> 'So what was the message you think you had about your grandmother burning all the papers the day before she died?'
> 'It seems as if there is a belief in your family that if you leave the alcoholic person completely alone at some point, in some way, they'll come out of it themselves? Where does this belief come from?'
> 'Do you think that your aunt devoting herself to your grandmother and always putting her parents first set up a pattern for how the youngest daughter should behave?'

Families have ways in which they respond to the scripts that are within their history. Some families just continue in the same way following the scripts exactly and hence they enact a *replicative script* as they try to replicate aspects of their family of origin in the family in which they live.

'What do you try to do the same in your family as you did in the family that you came from?'

Other families are at pains to do things so differently from their family of origin that they deliberately set out to construct ways of interacting that are the exact opposite to what they encountered during their childhood. These are known as *corrective scripts* and are seen when family members believe that they must contradict the script of the family of origin.

'What are you trying to do in your family that you want to do differently from how you did it in your family of origin?'

When addressing the 'level' of scripts, the therapist is seeking to both help families see what scripts are motivating their behaviour (constraining their repertoire of behaviour) and giving them the choice to change the script they are enacting. Byng-Hall (1995) calls these *improvised scripts*.

61

Letters to clients

There is a distinctive role for written correspondence in the essentially oral tradition of professional therapy (White and Epston 1990; Street and Downey 1996). Written communication has properties of form and meaning that make it distinct from the spoken word and, to some extent, autonomous from it. In particular written language tends to use a more precise grammar, more complete sentences, more clearly developed themes and a wider vocabulary than the spoken word. In writing to a family about the therapy, the author/therapist puts her thoughts and words into a concrete and static form and then puts them into the hands and ownership of the family. In doing so this correspondence may achieve something that is less easily managed in a conversation. It is important that a letter does not merely summarise what has occurred but is more of an extension of the conversation that has taken place between the therapist and family.

A letter about what is taking place in therapeutic sessions shifts the balance of relationship into one in which the family's independence from the therapist is emphasised and in which the autonomy to make whatever decisions they wish to is underscored. By making the family into a 'reader of words' such a letter places family members into observers or into a self-reflective position with regard to their own story. This assists them in seeing a fuller version of the difficulty and perhaps perceive new meanings or patterns in it. The letter does this in a public, open way that in itself provides a suitable punctuation point.

Letters are sent to clients at a variety of stages in therapy but the central aim is to summarise what has taken place and to set a particular frame on what could occur in the future. The letter will of course be written in a language that echoes the family's own language and ideology.

Within a letter particular issues need to be addressed:

- the problem that was initially referred
- the problem within its historical framework
- the issues around the problem, often using developmental terms
- a summary of the process of therapy sessions, including agreed elements of any contract or agenda
- clear statements about what the therapist and family could do jointly or what the family need to decide for themselves.

Dear Mr and Mrs Ryan

I am pleased that we have been able to meet to discuss the difficulty that you have been having with Lucy and the way in which the problems of going to bed and getting up in the middle of the night to come to you have caused such difficulties. As we discussed many things can go wrong in families when people lose their sleep as this does seem to make everything harder.

We discussed how you tried to find a solution to this problem but although there have been some changes at times this has been variable and you have never been certain that any change was due to what you were doing.

We have discussed the stages of a girl's development. As we talked about this we agreed that Lucy is very much in the stage of being a girl thinking about being a young woman but she is not yet a young woman and she is certainly not just a little girl. Clearly she has to struggle with some of the ideas about what being an independent person who takes responsibility for herself means.

As we have discussed it is difficult for parents with children in this stage of development to strike the right balance between gentle care and firmness. For you as a couple it has not necessarily been helpful for Mr Ryan to be the one to show the firmness and Mrs Ryan the gentle care. We certainly have reached a point when it is important for you to be able to jointly decide, at different times, whether Lucy requires a little more firmness or a little more gentle care. Should you as a couple decide whether it is the firm or gentle care route, I'm sure you will do this well. I know however that it has been difficult for you to have this discussion and it might well be that in the future we adults just need to talk about what stops you from jointly deciding on the best thing to do. Certainly the next few weeks will let us know how we should proceed in the future, and I look forward to meeting with you to find out what has happened.

Part 6

TECHNIQUES FROM SCHOOLS OF FAMILY THERAPY

62

Techniques from the strategic school of family therapy

Jay Haley (1973, 1976, 1980, 1981) was the founder of the strategic school of family therapy (Madanes 1981). His biography encompasses almost the full history of the field, from the pioneering days of Bateson at the Mental Research Institute (Fisch *et al.* 1982) to the 'established' days of the 2000s (Zeig 2001). His ideas, however, have a lot in common with the work of the MRI and so in this point we will 'conflate' both approaches.

The most frequently used techniques from this school are reframing and the use of paradox. Point 45 addresses reframing, therefore we will explore paradox in this point. A paradox is a contradictory statement that makes it hard to respond rationally. Examples of such paradoxes would be that the therapist at the end of every session would predict that the problem would emerge again and possibly would get worse. The strategic reasoning for this paradox would be that if the family expected the problem to get worse, then they would try harder to disprove the therapist and make sure they succeeded, not fail. If, however, it did get worse, this proved how competent, if not prescient, the therapist was and they would be more likely to do as she asked next time.

From a critical standpoint, we can see why such interventions are often seen as disrespectful and therefore not possible in contemporary practice. However, 'predicting relapse', as it was called, can still play a part in family therapy. The therapist might do this because she knows it will empower the family rather than wanting to be shown to be clever. She also may 'play' with the idea: '*I think you have all done really well to turn this problem around, but I don't think we have heard the last of this problem. I wouldn't be surprised if it came back to trick you all; what could you do even more to stop this happening?*' It is also true that a therapist may choose to warn families that the problem might re-occur, especially when they are convinced that they have overcome it. In this case the therapist is 'inoculating' the family so that disappointment does not sap their resolve in future. In these instances, the technique of predicting relapse is useful.

This is also true of other paradoxical interventions that Haley frequently adopted, such as having family members change their family roles. Haley demonstrated this technique in a video in which he asked the 'good' child to pretend to be the 'bad' child for a couple of weeks: '*I am wondering whether you would be willing to try an experiment for me? Could you see, just for a week, if you could swap roles? So you who are always good see if you can learn to be bad, then maybe your bad brother might learn to be good!*' The intention in such an intervention is not to outsmart the family but to find any strategic intervention that will help the family move in the direction they wish to move in. Here, the assumption is that family patterns have 'made' one child 'good' and one child 'bad'. In a systemic sense, the bad relies on the good and vice versa. So by experimenting with opposite behaviour, the children learn that they can be themselves, act as they choose and bring behaviour they thought was out of their control into their control. In contemporary practice such paradoxes can be used if they are explored in a playful way, particularly in the later stages of therapy.

Strategic interventions are often motivated by the idea that habitual patterns build up over time and that often the patterns that are designed to solve a problem simply then become the problem. An example would be a family who adopt a punitive intervention to stop their 3-year-old from having tantrums. If they try this more and more, in many cases it will not only make the tantrums worse, but will add new problems: partner conflict, family stress, feelings of incompetence, etc. Deriving his ideas from Milton Erickson (Haley 1973), Haley argued that in such situations the task of the therapist was to interrupt this habitual cycle of behaviour in any way at all.

One common intervention when parents disagreed about how to handle such a child might be to ask the father to decide on the odd days of the week and the mother to decide on the even days. On the last day they had to toss a coin to decide who was 'in charge'. This task could be used in similar situations today even if the quality of the relationship between therapist and family was collaborative. In such situations, the therapist might tentatively broach the idea of a *'crazy task that has helped some families in the past but may not suit your family'*. The therapist would explain that the purpose is to change the pattern so that the family are free to choose whatever they want to do rather than be tricked into acting the way they always have.

63

Techniques from structural family therapy

We have already included some of the most significant contributions to family therapy practice from structural family therapy within the earlier points. Minuchin (1974; Minuchin and Fishman 1981), the founder of structural family therapy, established the concepts of family adaptability and cohesion (Point 46) and also used enactment (Point 58). His understanding of families was centred upon their structure. This concept described a number of dimensions, including the cohesion of the family (emotional closeness), their ability to adapt to the changing needs of the family's members (adaptability) and the hierarchy (who has the power) of the family. Minuchin argued that families with problems often seemed to have incoherent structures when it came to cohesion, hierarchy or ability to adapt.

Structural family therapy is often viewed as having a particular active 'style', sometimes interpreted as confrontational. Structural family therapists will frequently move about in the room. Sometimes they might sit on the floor next to a family member who is either struggling with the topics discussed or needs encouragement to take part. Sometimes the 'body' of the therapist is used to block what the therapist feels are unhelpful communications (such as a parent interrupting what a child has to say). Sometimes, the therapist uses her body to 'protect' a conversation from interruptions (such as a conversation between siblings about their parents, which their parents may want to influence). Structural family therapists use space and physical closeness to 'mark' out both current family patterns and also to change them: '*I notice that every time we meet, your daughter sits between her parents. Let's see how we all feel if we have her sitting over here and not between you.*'

Therapists will explain why they do this in a number of ways. Such as: '*I want everyone to speak for themselves and feel able to do so without others interrupting them, so it helps to avoid too much eye contact, which means sometimes I might ask you to change places'* or *'Do you know, it feels like I am watching a tennis match here: going from Mum to Dad to Dad to Mum. It would be easier on my neck if you both sat together: would you mind moving like that?'* In this way a structural approach is more active in the way that it observes the interaction that takes place in the room.

Predominantly, the approach will want families to practice behavioural changes in the therapy room with the expectation that these will continue when the family go home. An example of this is that the therapist will *restructure* the family by *unbalancing* coalitions that she thinks are unhelpful: *'You know I sometimes think you are just too helpful to your daughter. Can you practice for me, not speaking for her. Just try. I know it will be hard. Maybe, just maybe, you will learn a little about what she really needs you to do.'*

With some structural techniques the therapist asks the family to role-play typical situations at home in order to push them to find an alternative result. This version of enactment is called *intensification.*

Therapist:	I do not believe that you are saying what you really want to, to your Dad. Come on be honest: tell him what you want him to do.
Daughter:	I can't. He will be upset.
Therapist:	Of course he will be upset. That is what parents are for isn't it? To be upset by what their children say. Tell me are you frightened that he will go crazy or something?
Daughter:	No I. . . .
Therapist:	Well what is it. Don't let this feeling shut you up. It can't be good to live like that.
Daughter:	I am not frightened about what he will do but what he will feel.
Therapist:	Ah, you think he will sulk?
Daughter:	I don't know. . . . no. . . . it will hurt him so bad he will start drinking again.

Here we can see that the therapist intensifies the emotional tension in order to help a family member state what may have been an unwritten rule that determined family behaviour.

In *unbalancing* the therapist supports one family member in order to challenge the whole family into changing. For instance, in the situation of a child who is having temper tantrums, the therapist might support the child.

Therapist:	So who is the boss in your family Ginny?
Ginny (6-year-old):	I am.
Therapist:	Oh I am glad we have sorted that out. You know I have learnt that only if I talk to the boss of the family can I help. So let's just ignore Mum and Dad at the moment shall we? You and I will work out what they have to do.

Clearly, the therapist does not believe that this is how a family should be! But the unbalancing intervention is designed to challenge the child's mother and father to change the way they treat their 6-year-old.

64

Techniques from solution-focused family therapy

Solution-focused therapy began within family therapy and integrated many family therapy concepts and techniques within its work (de Shazer 1982, 1985, 1988). However, the current solution-focused literature tends to have an emphasis upon work with individuals rather than with couples or family groups. Despite this many solution-focused techniques are a regular part of family therapy practice, albeit with a relationship focus.

Solution-focused therapy argues that individuals and families should do more of what works rather than concentrate upon the 'problems' they have, hence it is more 'present' and 'solution' based than most family therapies.

So in the first session one technique is to ask what the family have done already that has made a positive difference: '*I start my sessions by asking not what is the problem that has brought you to see me today, but what have you noticed works already that makes the problem better?*'

This is followed up by asking all family members to comment. Such an approach immediately encourages a view within the family about resources, solutions and capability rather than defeat, failure and difficulty. Of course, solution-focused therapy does not want to hear about any solution: The solution needs to be realistic, describable and attainable. One way in which solution-focused therapists help families reach a description of the solution is to ask what has been called *the miracle question*: '*Suppose one night you were all asleep and a miracle happened and you all woke up and the problem was solved. How would you know? What would be different? Who would notice first and what would they notice? Who would be next? Who would be most surprised/pleased?*'

The therapist however has to help family members describe changes in a concrete manner: The expectation is that if they can be envisaged then they are more achievable. Sometimes family members may struggle to come up with an answer to the miracle question. In this case, the therapist needs to help them look at what happened when the problem was not present.

> *Therapist*: Can you think of an example when Ginny started to have a tantrum and stopped?
>
> *Mother*: Yes, the other day, I said no to her having an ice cream and I expected her to kick off, but she didn't. It was quite funny, she sort of seemed to think about it and then just kind of got on with it.

These are called '*exceptions*' and the therapist uses them to explore what the family did or what was happening at the time so that these times can be expanded.

'*Scaling*' seeks to use the metaphorical language of degree in applying to all 'problem' or 'solution' situations: '*So on a scale of 1 to 10 in which 10 is the worst tantrum Ginny has ever had, how "bad" was that one?*' The purpose of scaling is not however to 'fix' something in stone, but rather to explore difference: '*So it was a 5. OK what made it a 5 and not say a 6 or a 4?*'

Once more the intention is to build a knowledge of what makes things change for the better and lead the family towards a life that is not bothered by the issue that brought them to therapy. In some family therapy sessions, the therapist can employ scaling interactively by asking who is most confident that the problem can be resolved. This would lead onto enacting a conversation between the most hopeful person and the least hopeful, with the intention of increasing solution talk and of course creating motivation within the family system for change.

65

Techniques from narrative family therapy

Michael White (White and Epston 1990; White 1995; White 2007), one of the founders of narrative therapy, initially trained in the Milan school of family therapy but he became increasingly uncomfortable with the systems metaphor and adopted a narrative one as the bedrock of his therapy. Most contemporary family therapists use narrative techniques even if they do not necessarily agree with the whole philosophy of the approach.

Narrative therapists use the metaphor of narrative as their main working concept rather than 'systems'. Such an approach allows the therapist to begin exploring the story that a family presents and seeks to alter not the relational aspects of the story, as a traditional family therapist would do, but the *relativistic elements of the story* itself. Narrative therapists argue that human problems are the product of choosing a narrative that leads to difficulties when actually there are a multiple number of narratives to choose from, many of which can be positive. Narrative practice therefore is about finding these more positive narratives and using them as alternatives. Clearly, this is not a simple process and requires attention to language and description. The narrative therapist listens to the narrative of the family and looks for *subjugated* narratives: these are ones where the family have resisted the *dominant* narrative that will be problem focused. Often, White found that the dominant narrative was based in a societal level of context. An example would be that some young women are obsessed with weight and therefore get described as anorexic. A narrative therapist would be interested in talking to such a young woman about where the idea that women should be thin came from. Then she might see if the client had ever resisted that idea. Such a new subjugated narrative would then be bolstered by the involvement of others (often, but not only, family members) who could support this new narrative.

A similar process would be used in the situation referred to above where a family comes to therapy wanting help with their 6-year-old daughter who is having 'tantrums'. A dominant discourse here might be that 'mothers/women are better parents especially when it comes to bringing up girls'. This may mean that Ginny's father leaves all the child care to his partner and feels inadequate when he tries to help because Ginny rejects his intervention more than she rejects her mother's. Her mother on the other hand feels that she is a failure as Ginny seems unhappy whatever she does for her, so she feels that the dominant discourse proves that she is not a good mother. Within this scenario, the *subjugated* discourse is one that resists the pressure of 'truth' within the dominant discourse. Here, for instance, this might be Ginny's mother's anger at being left to be the 'perfect mother' who never gets her own needs met. Thus a narrative therapist would be keen to help family members work out which narrative they would wish to live by, rather than being dominated by the idea that there is a 'norm'. White called the moments when the subjugated discourse emerged 'sparkling moments' or unique outcomes, and he would talk about these very diligently in his therapy.

This narrative understanding has also led to the assertion that *the person is not the problem, rather the problem is the problem*. In some senses this is again another more complex reframing technique that aims to prevent individuals feeling blamed for what is 'going wrong'. However, within narrative therapy this has become the axiom that supports the technique of *externalisation*. This is a meticulous process in which the therapist helps the family or individual build up a picture of how the problem in question affects their lives and gradually gives this external entity a description and an identity.

> *Therapist*: So tell me Ginny, what should we call these tantrums? Do you have a helpful way of describing them to us? I know that some children I have worked with have called them 'monster moments'.
>
> *Ginny*: Yes when Mummy talks about them she calls them my Habdabs.

> *Therapist*: That is a good name for them. . . . mmm Habdabs. Can we have a conversation about how these Habdabs take over your life?

The conversation would then begin to map the strength of the 'Habdabs', how they affect each family member, when Ginny is able to resist the power of the 'Habdabs' and what help she would like to have from other people to resist them more. Narrative therapists describe this process as the *scaffolding* of the externalisation: the gradual building up of a conversation in which all family members are drawn into uniting to change the narrative that has dominated them for so long. In this process, questions are asked about the '*landscape of action*' that will help the family map how the problem prevents them from being who they want to be and will help them discover unique outcomes. *Landscape of consciousness questions* will explore how the problem limits what people can think.

Narrative therapy is possibly the most creative development within family therapy in the last 20 years. Many of its techniques are used by family therapists although, as a form of therapy, it is increasingly independent of family therapy. Indeed, more recently, it has become a 'subgroup' within the counselling profession (McLeod 1997; Payne 2006).

66

Techniques from attachment-based therapies

Attachment-based understandings and techniques have always had a place within family therapy (Byng-Hall 1995). The earlier view predominantly drew on ideas that explained that the role of the therapist was to create a safe space within the therapy to enable families to explore difficult emotions. It was further suggested that the therapist actually became an attachment figure for family members. The development of attachment-based ideas in therapy, however, has taken the discussion to a more complex level. Hughes (2007) for example has promulgated *attachment-focused family therapy* where the therapist must seek to repair any attachment 'damage' by modelling being a secure attachment figure. She also teaches both child and parent the fundamental social skills that are learnt through an appropriate attachment bond. These include the ability to be empathic, to be reflective, to understand emotions and to attune to other human beings. The therapist aims to embody these capabilities and enables a conversation to occur that helps the family learn these skills. This process begins with the therapist entering the world of the family by matching her affective style to that of the family. Drawing upon ideas about how children learn to be socially competent, Hughes (2007) describes therapists as leading parents and children into dialogues that allow for the regulation of strong emotions and encourage reflection upon experience.

In the example of a young woman who had been distressed that her mother had not been available to her whilst she was a teenager:

Therapist: Sarah, you said you felt alone during those times when your mother could not cope; tell us what it felt like.

Sarah: Well, I would go to school and know that when I came home Mum would be drunk or in bed and just unable to cope and I would wish I had been able to live with Dad or something and I only wanted to be normal.

Therapist: That must have been difficult. What did you feel . . . can you tell us?

Sarah: I just said, I was upset.

Therapist: I guess I would have been scared that I had to look after my Mum. Maybe she would die and leave me on my own. Maybe I was also angry at her but scared to say in case she killed herself and did leave me on my own. If that happened, who would look after me?

Sarah: I wasn't angry but I am now when I see what she has done to me.

Therapist: (*Turning to Sarah's mother*) This must be hard to hear. Do you think you can hear what your daughter says, or do you find yourself not listening or trying to stop her by saying 'you don't understand'?

Mother: It is hard and I do want to say 'don't you remember the good times we had together?'.

Therapist: I know you want to say that, but what do you think your daughter needs to hear from you to be able to move on from that feeling of hurt and anger?

This excerpt demonstrates how an attachment focus can help therapists structure their interventions to help families model affect regulation and reflexiveness about the other.

There are a number of other attachment-focused perspectives on family therapy, many of which construct significant family interventions on attachment theory (Kozlowska and Hanney 2001; Dallos 2004, 2006; May 2005; Vetere and Dallos 2008). Dallos (2006) and Vetere and Dallos (2008) combine narrative therapy ideas with attachment theory to provide a model of family therapy. These UK authors emphasise the role of 'soothing' interactions in family life that build up an individual's ability to cope with difficult life events and emotions. They therefore structure their *attachment narrative therapy* to elicit such soothing. The advantage of such a narrative systemic approach to attachment therapy is that it avoids the overly deterministic implications of some interpretations of attachment theory, as it postulates that even the 'narratives' of attachment are available for narrative change. It also opens up attachment theory to a whole family perspective rather than the traditional mother–child dyad.

67

Techniques from psycho-educational approaches

Within contemporary family therapy practice there is an increasing role for 'cross-fertilisation' from different therapeutic modalities. There is also an increasing 'working alongside' other professions and a strong influence of evidence-based practice (Rivett 2008). Within this context, there have been some quite startling changes to the way family therapists understand and talk about issues that have traditionally been the preserve of medical practitioners. This change is no more clear than in the field of adult mental health, especially that of psychosis. The early family therapists such as Haley and Bateson understood psychosis as being understandable within the family context but also ascribed causative and functional characteristics to family dynamics and psychosis. These ideas were heavily criticised by a number of psychiatric researchers and largely proved to be simplistic in terms of their understanding about the 'cause' of mental illness. Moreover they were interpreted as blaming the family for the illness of the young person. In response to this, research suggested that there was a place for 'communication' training with families of schizophrenic young people (Kuipers et al. 1999) and that this training could reduce relapse rates. This research centred upon the emotional interaction between family members. Across a number of rigorous studies it was concluded that the level of 'expressed emotion' between family members could be correlated to levels of relapse (Leff et al. 1982). Specifically, the degree of expressed hostility and criticism seemed to be crucial. Therefore, these 'family management' interventions concentrated upon teaching family members about mental illness and helped them communicate with each other with less hostility and criticism. Family therapists in this and other specialties have accepted these findings and incorporated them into their practice (Burbach and Stanbridge 1998, 2006; Fadden 1998).

A large component of the 'family management' intervention packages is that families are taught about how psychosis manifests, what can trigger it and what coping strategies they need to adopt to prevent relapse. Clearly there are a number of challenges within this way of working that challenge some of the basic axioms of family therapy. These include the use of a 'firm' label for a problem when family therapy seeks to place such labels in context and thus lessen their power. Family management techniques also almost always teach that psychosis is a biological illness when traditionally family therapy avoids such 'totalising' descriptions.

However, with the use of relapse prevention strategies, the family management approach can also be seen as opening up the possibility to change even within such a dominant medical description. It seeks to empower families with their 'ill' person and, just like family therapy, seeks to harness the family's resources to make changes in family life. It is therefore not surprising that family therapists in a number of specialties have now incorporated some of the family management or 'psycho-educational approaches', as they are called, into their practice. Most family therapists working in adult mental health will explore what 'story' about the illness fits for the family and will also describe the 'expressed emotion' research in order to help the family adapt and challenge some of the negative consequences of psychosis: *Tell me which way of understanding John's illness fits for you? Do you sometimes think that you muddle behaviour that is "just John" rather than "John's illness"?*

These uses of psycho-educational approaches assume that the therapist does 'know' some 'facts' from research and clinical practice. Not surprisingly some family therapists would rather leave such discussions to other professionals in the multi-disciplinary team but, equally, many would be happy to explore these ideas and use their relationship with the family to develop a shared understanding about the illness and how to manage it. Psycho-educational approaches have also influenced family therapy practice in settings such as parent training and in work with eating disorders.

Part 7

ENDING THERAPY

Reviewing progress

In family therapy, because the general process is one of assisting the family to reflect on themselves, it is implicit that the therapist will check constantly where the family are in relation to their problem and their experience of the therapy. Although the issues discussed will have ranged far and wide in an attempt to make changes that influence the family system, the presenting problem in the way that it is reflected in the family's mandate to the therapist is the reference point to which the therapist needs to return. As Pinsof (1983) notes, the problem/intervention link does not always have to be direct and obvious but the process of sponsoring change must always be conceptually tied to the problem and its resolution. By inviting the family to review and reflect on this mandate, the therapist encourages a self-monitoring process, which at some point will lead to the termination process. Not only does the family need to monitor its own performance but the therapist also needs to develop the means and techniques of reviewing her own behaviour so that the direction of therapy is maintained.

Progress is monitored at the beginning of the session by the therapist asking the family '*How are things going?*' Depending on the content of the reply, this is then followed up with clarifying questions: '*What happened that told you things were better/worse?*', '*Were there any good/bad events last week?*' It is preferable not to enquire directly about the presenting problem per se but to ask about those interactions that have been established as being related to the presenting problem. Once such information has been elicited the therapist's task is to seek interactional reports on what has occurred between sessions in order to support family members' perceptions of progress.

For example, in the case of the Davies family (Point 56 onwards), the task was for Mr Davies to visit his son and report back to his wife on how he felt about it and have the daughter just observe her parents after the visit had happened. So here the therapist would ask Mr Davies how his visit went and then ask Mrs Davies how her husband reported to her what had happened and then ask Mr Davies to comment on his wife's description. The therapist would enquire of the daughter how she saw this particular interaction and ask the parents whether or not she just maintained an observer role. As with any interactional report the therapist will always establish some of the interactions that occurred prior to and following those being focused on: '*How did your husband lead up to telling you what happened?*' '*What did you all do when you had finished talking about it?*'. By this means each person's perception of what happened is openly discussed and placed within the context of their general interaction. The therapist tracks interaction in such a way that the family can appreciate those elements of their behaviour that make a difference and those elements that were helpful in securing a positive outcome. This then forms the basis of monitoring with regard to the therapist's mandate, namely whether or not family arguments were lessened. Thus the therapist might finish this sequence with the question: '*How has this task helped/not helped lessen family conflict? Is it worth trying it again?*'

69

Termination

It is important when considering termination in family therapy that the view of the flowing interactive nature of family life is maintained. Termination implies that something is being ended and hence whatever was happening before will cease to happen after; however, in terms of a systemic notion of change, the difference between before and after therapy sessions does not mean that the interactive change process embarked on will also cease. To put this another way: The endpoint of family work is difficult to define because the notion of the family life cycle cuts across the idea that the family is ever in a 'correct' state; it is in continual movement and the notion of a set of circumstances that can be identified as 'cure' is impossible to sustain. Encouraging families to monitor their own health and their own need for ongoing help allows some to choose an entry-exit-entry-exit sequence of contact with their therapist. If such a pattern appears, provided the family are not just repeating the same process over and over again, we may consider that the idea of a 'termination' should be best termed 'terminations', with all that this implies. Indeed as the process of monitoring is a core feature of the session to session process, the questions posed from the monitoring position continually present to the family a potential discussion about ceasing the ongoing contact. The family is responsible for terminating therapy, and by accurately listening the therapist will be able to open the discussion into one where ceasing contact becomes the theme. In doing this a particular set of questions follow:

'What happened to the problem?'
'How do the family explain this occurrence?'
'What was the role of everybody in this change?'
'If a similar problem emerged again, what would the family do?'

'Why do the family think it happened in the first place?'
'Are the family clear that they wish to cease sessions?'
'What would be a sign that the family need to return to the therapist?'

With these questions the therapist supports the family's decision about termination and reinforces their view about this. All families benefit from having a full discussion about termination because this helps them maintain a 'public' awareness of how they go about dealing with their difficulties. Whatever the changes outlined by the family, the therapist is then able to reinforce the differences that have been made and their approach to problems. Throughout this, the therapist is continually orientated towards the future so that the seed is sown about the possibility of problems in time to come – problems that can be faced without trepidation and without the thought that failure has occurred. By reinforcing the way in which the family have discussed change between themselves and with herself, the therapist provides the family with a 'ghost' of herself – an image not so much of the person but of the activity that was undertaken to confront and overcome their difficulties. The therapist is now within the family's collective memory – she has become part of their story and in her struggle to become an effective therapist they have become part of hers.

During the termination stage of therapy, the therapist will want to help the family describe any 'relapse prevention' strategies they would like to use. She may also suggest (in a strategic way) that the family should manufacture a minor 'problem' to prove they can cope with things before termination.

70

Early termination

It is not unusual for families to simply stop attending family therapy with no explanation or warning. There may be a number of reasons for this and some of them are not the obvious ones. For instance, when this happens a family therapist may assume that the family have 'relapsed' and decided that the therapy is not working. In fact research has suggested that success is as likely a cause of not attending as failure: Families just do not see the need to continue (Hubble *et al.* 2000). From one perspective this is fine: It is better to get on with life and not be constrained by 'problem' stories than continue with therapy. However, for the therapist this can be extremely frustrating. It is therefore important that 'how we stop working together' becomes a theme in the initial meeting where a contract for work is arranged. Usually, it is agreed that families contact the therapist if they no longer wish to keep an appointment.

If families do stop attending with no warning, it is therefore useful for the therapist to reflect upon what has happened and make contact with the family themselves rather than assuming there has been a relapse or there has been a resurgence of 'normal life'. This raises issues about the self of the therapist as some therapists want to be 'wanted' and some want to be 'successful'. These desires may have their roots in childhood and family scripts. Having a family stop can be an opportunity to reflect upon these. It is also very humbling to hear from a family that, for instance, they moved house and suddenly all problems evaporated. A sceptical therapist might doubt this but again, given that systems theory suggests that changes can come about from any contextual change, it is a possible cause of family improvements.

Many organisations will have set procedures for this early termination. Some will make contact with a family in a bureaucratic manner with a standard letter. In private practice most therapists will ring the family, especially as a financial cost may be incurred from failing to attend without warning. It is also the case that busy clinicians will not routinely make direct contact in such situations, which is less helpful both for the therapist, who can learn about her practice from such contacts, and for the family.

71

Follow-up

As families come to indicate that they are considering termination it may be appropriate for the therapist to suggest that there be a follow-up appointment, which naturally contains the idea that the 'next one' could be the 'last one'. For some families, a set of follow-up appointments serves as a way of maintaining involvement in the therapeutic process, whereas for other families one follow-up appointment is exactly what it says – a one-off appointment to see how things are going. Some therapists at the outset of therapy establish a contract in which it is agreed with the family beforehand that when the therapy sessions are deemed to have finished then there will be a follow-up appointment some months later. Different families and different contexts of therapy require different approaches from therapists and how follow-up appointments are arranged with a particular family would clearly need negotiation with them. Research has indicated that planned follow-up appointments at a three-month distance can have a productive therapeutic impact (Street and Downey 1996), particularly if it is presented as an integral part of the process during the initial meeting. Therefore it is beneficial for therapists to indicate the value of such a follow-up.

Treacher (1989) has identified different categories of follow-up:

- *The safety net*. This is where the family are uncertain about their change process and would like to have the reassurance of having a follow-up at some point.
- *The routine check*. This is a more matter-of-fact follow-up along the lines of 'let's meet again in three months' just to check out what is happening.
- *Telephone follow-up*. For some families a brief telephone call can serve instead of an interview. This is a useful strategy

when therapy has gone well and where there may not be a need for a full family session. In some cases a follow-up appointment can be made and the family informed that they can telephone to cancel the appointment if they consider it is not necessary to attend. Such a strategy also allows the family to be aware that the therapist is still available to them.

- *Failure follow-up*. This is a follow-up where the therapist finds some way of contacting the family that fails to attend. This may be an enquiry letter, a telephone call or a request of the referring agents. Therapists should give considerable thought to this type of follow-up as it is important that the only message the family receives is about the continuing availability of therapeutic sessions.

- *The research follow-up*. Therapists and agencies do need to evaluate their effectiveness and a variety of formal and informal staff members exist for this. Contact of this nature should be planned well in advance of termination in order for it to be beneficial to the family. There is a tradition in family therapy that the therapist or a colleague conducts an interview of this sort in order to help develop practice.

72

Assessment of outcome

Above we have noted that therapists and agencies can have formal processes by which they monitor the effectiveness of the work done. Sometimes this merges into empirical research. There is always an issue in therapeutic practice of how outcome should be assessed and whether this should rely on clinical judgement, family view or whether it requires an empirical process. It is important to distinguish between the two types of research activity and clinical practice. Certainly the role and function of research in clinical practice need to be recognised as they are central in the development of practice, but the correspondence between the aims of researchers and practitioners is more apparent than real. Their activities in achieving the aim of shedding light on questions about best practice are not the same. They adopt methods that best address their particular lines of enquiry and although the fields are interested in the same phenomena each is constructed and equipped to answer different questions (Rivett and Street 2003): one through the application of psychotherapy in its clinical context and the other through the strategy of protocols and methods aimed at obtaining data and testing hypotheses. In developing a therapeutic practice it must be recognised that in the last analysis the requirements of the therapists should predominate.

The priority of researchers in clinical trials is to demonstrate an underlying causal relationship between the intervention and, hopefully, improvement. The researcher requires tight controls on the way the treatment is structured and administered, the way the sample is selected and how outcomes are assessed. By contrast, the therapist's priority is more pragmatic, being less concerned with the demonstration of the value of specific components and more interested in the process towards the final outcome (Sexton *et al.* 2008).

Despite the differences in orientation researchers have provided a background with which to evaluate family therapy and there have been a number of excellent reviews of the research literature in recent years (Gurman *et al.* 1986; Friedlander *et al.* 1994; Pinsof and Wynne 1995; Friedlander 1998; Carr 2009a, 2009b). Pinsof and Wynne (1995) have provided a number of substantive conclusions that outline the contribution of family therapy:

1　Family therapy works.
2　Family therapy is not harmful.
3　Family therapy is more efficacious than standard and/or individual treatment for specific conditions (including adult schizophrenia; depressed outpatient women in distressed marriages; marital distress; adult alcoholism and drug abuse; adolescent drug abuse; adolescent conduct disorders; anorexia in young adolescent females; and various chronic physical illnesses in adults and children).
4　There are no scientific data at this time to support the superiority of any particular form of family therapy over any other.
5　Family therapy is not sufficient in itself to treat effectively a variety of severe disorders and problems.

Regardless of this it is important to recognise the specific orientation of a therapist. The skill of the 'good' therapist lies in his or her ability to detect obstacles that would make it difficult to implement a therapy and to make the adaptation necessary to aid the clients. In other words a therapist should have the capacity to monitor and maintain the therapeutic alliance in the face of all the problems of everyday practice. These are obstacles that the researcher attempts to eliminate. There is a risk that the sophistication of research trials that demand clear causal influence can overregulate therapy content and underemphasise the freedom of action available to individual therapists (Roth and Fonagy, 1996). The task of applying research findings to daily clinical practice calls for the capacity on the part of the therapist to see the pertinence of specific discoveries to the individual case. It is in the application of the general to the individual that marks out the skilful clinician.

Part 8

THE SELF OF THE THERAPIST

73

Congruence – the use of self

In order to be curious about a family as well as actively occupying a neutral non-judgemental position (and certainly not taking sides), it is necessary for the therapist to be present as a 'self': to be congruent. This involves being able to make 'use of the self'. This firstly involves accepting one's self as a fellow human being who is personally offering something more than mere technical professional expertise. This does not negate professional ethical requirements and competencies but adds an extra dimension: personal caring, which is itself contained within the boundary of that professional behaviour. All therapists need to be able to communicate in a genuine way that this particular encounter with this particular family is important to them and that there is a personal commitment to that encounter.

'Use of self' also involves being aware and acknowledging to oneself that each of us have personal vulnerabilities and capabilities and as a therapist these are present in the encounter, but not in a way that interferes with the therapeutic process. This type of awareness and acknowledgement provides a personal clarity that informs the therapist about which part of the self to share and which to withhold in order to retain one's own integrity whilst encountering clients. It is important that all of us are aware that we experience pain and difficulty about many issues and similarly it is equally important that we are aware of what issues need to be kept to ourselves.

At its basic, 'use of self' refers to that straightforward process of checking out one's own reactions to what is going on, and then reflecting and sharing one's own thoughts about what is happening in the therapy room. A part of this process is appreciating that this needs to be done in a helpful way rather than dominating the session with one's own thoughts and feelings.

Implicit in the idea of the 'use of self' is an awareness of 'who you are' as this helps the therapist determine which clients she will be best able to serve and also which particular interventive strategies are likely to be most useful in any particular occasion. There is no 'right' or 'wrong' way of making use of self apart from the fact that the therapist does need to be congruent with herself in the room at any one moment. Indeed within this continuum each therapist will not find their own 'permanent' position because within different contexts and with different families different therapist skills and hence different therapist 'selves' will be called upon, and these will be the 'self' that best fits the experience of the therapy at that moment. This view of self is what differentiates family therapy and systemic practice from many of the individual therapies: The systemic self is fluctuating, it is not a static 'true' self.

Congruence of a therapist within family therapy means that within the relationships of the therapy the therapist is freely and deeply herself, with this experience accurately represented in awareness. This means that the therapist consciously interacts with the family in a way that is determined by her choices of interaction and she does not allow herself to follow the family's preferences for interaction except where she does so as a matter of conscious choice. The therapist should be able to monitor her own actions and feelings so that she can detect when she is inappropriately reciprocating family interactions or introducing personal emotions, thoughts and behaviours that have no place at this juncture. Congruence is therefore related to knowing what is required personally and what is not required personally. To be congruent the therapist should experience the feeling '*I am freely able to attempt to interact in a way that I choose and use what comes up for me in a way that is helpful for the family*'.

74

The therapist's own family scripts

One aspect of the self that has always been regarded as important for the family therapist is that she understands her own family scripts (Lieberman 1987; Simon 1989; Lerner 1999; Haber and Hawley 2004). This is important as, without being aware of such scripts, the therapist may find herself 'pulled into' unhelpful family scripts in the families she works with. For instance, it is not unusual for therapists who are not parents to find they naturally 'side' with the children, especially if the family dynamic is understood as one in which the children are resisting the rules of the parents. Family therapists are therefore taught to analyse their own role in their family of origins and recognise how they have interpreted family life from this stance (for an autobiographical account, see Street 1989). Some theorists have called these kinds of assumptions 'prejudices' (Cecchin and Lane 1991) and have encouraged family therapists to remain irreverent or curious about them so that they can control their influence on the therapy. These influences might also come not from past family scripts but from current (family of creation) ones. For instance, when a therapist suffers a bereavement, she may find herself avoiding mentioning loss in family sessions with families at exactly the point at which it would be useful to do so. These dynamics will often surface in supervision when difficulties working with a family are described. As such difficulties are deconstructed, it will often turn out to be a situation that echoes the therapist's own family situation.

Often, we find that those who are naturally attracted to family therapy have spent a childhood in an 'observer' role within their own families. Thus they might already have a natural inquisitiveness about their own family and it is not unusual to find them reflecting that they were almost already in the 'therapy role' by the time they reached adolescence. In some cases, the 'therapist to be' will be the confidante of one parent. Another common scenario is that the therapist was the youngest child of their family. This birth position (Sulloway 1997) often carries a feeling of being separate from the other siblings and often 'special' to the parents. All these scripts raise issues that the therapy 'system' has to address so that it does not become biased during therapy.

Family therapy has approached these issues in a number of ways. We have highlighted that therapists during their training and professional life are required to address their own scripts via self-reflection and supervision, but the use of teams is an additional aide in attending to these concerns. Again, it is common practice for a family therapy team, when it first convenes, to work together to consider each member's family tree so that they can understand how these will influence the team dynamic as well as the therapy process. For instance, one team that undertook this work discovered that although two team members were youngest children (Rivett *et al.* 1997), one had had 'responsibility' thrust upon him whilst the other had been the 'irresponsible' family member. Not surprisingly, these two tended to fall easily into a competitive interaction in which one (the 'responsible' one) wanted to control the team process whilst the other (the 'irresponsible' one) wanted more creativity and freedom. The other dynamic in this team was that other team members were women who were both older daughters. Thus a gender dynamic existed within the team: The women 'observed' the younger boys, who competed between each other. This dynamic remained a constant issue for the team as it worked with families. In such situations, the drawing of parallels between family scripts, team behaviour and therapeutic process can allow for difference and the development of new scripts.

The dimension of gender and its pervasive influence upon family life is a crucial element in family therapists understanding who they are as therapists. Family therapists need to cultivate a distance from the messages about gender and gender stereotypes that they have learnt in childhood. For some men and women these messages become 'scripts' that they may seek to correct in adult life, or they may have internalised many ideas about how men and women should be in intimate relationships that influence the ways they think about the families they work with. Thus their own definition of themselves as gendered and sexually orientated individuals must be available for consideration. Moreover, therapists are not immune to the dynamics between fathers, mothers, sons and daughters (Silverstein and Rashbaum 1994). For instance, many therapists may have been closer to one gendered parent or other. In 'straight' relationships this might lead to a preference to listening to the voice of men or to women. If there has been a troubled relationship with one parent, then this may translate into critical interactions with the parent in therapy who 'represents' that parent. Family therapy literature has particularly noted that on the one hand men's voices appear to be privileged in therapy (Dienhart 2001), whilst on the other hand men are often not involved enough in therapy (Featherstone *et al.* 2007). This may be connected to the gender scripts of the therapists as much as it is connected to social stereotypes.

This concentration on gender also has repercussions for diversity practice. Therapists who hold very rigid views about either gender or sexual orientation are likely to be unable to provide the appropriate therapeutic help for families in which there is diversity on these issues. Thus a female therapist who held a strong view that 'all women should work outside the home' might be unable to respect the views of some women who choose to work in the home while children are small. Equally, a therapist who held firm views about gay and lesbian relationships would be unable to help such families who were seeking therapy. It is therefore also part of the 'self' of the therapist that opinions and attitudes are available for reflection and challenge.

75

Developing a therapeutic presence

Family therapy is a personally demanding form of therapy. The therapist needs to be alert to verbal and non-verbal interactions in the room and has to be able to manage a complex multi-voiced conversation. In learning to do this, therapists need to develop a form of presence so that they can be present within the conversation but not dominate it. Although it is difficult to describe what therapeutic presence is for family therapists, we would suggest that it is demonstrated by a poise and purpose in how a therapist behaves and intervenes in the ongoing session. There are perhaps three aspects to this presence that are particularly significant. The first is to have the confidence to intervene quite firmly if required. As family therapy sessions can be fast moving and entail multiple themes, it is not unusual for family members to talk over each other, to disqualify what another says or even to ignore the content of what a family member has said. The family therapist in such situations must manage the session such that members hear each other and listen to the content of what is said.

Mother:	All she ever does is go out and come back late.
Daughter:	I can't stand to be at home.
Mother:	I wait up and wait up and get scared something has happened to her.
Therapist:	I wonder if you heard what your daughter said just now: she can't stand to be at home.
Mother:	That's rubbish. She likes to get drunk and stuff.
Therapist:	OK but if she meant that, why would she be feeling so bad about being at home?

In this example, the therapist needs to be alert to the contribution of family members but also able to 'punctuate' the conversation. These skills are usually experienced by therapists trained in individual work as much more active and forceful than their usual practice. For work with families, therapists need to have the confidence to monitor and steer the conversation in a therapeutically helpful direction whilst maintaining an active involvement with the ongoing process.

Secondly, the poise or presence of the family therapist is made up of an understanding about what kinds of conversation will be therapeutically helpful. Schon (1983) hypothesised that professionals incorporated a multitude of knowledge in their practice that is as much reliant on experience and reflection on that experience as it is on theory. In terms of family therapy, clearly therapeutic presence is more than simply transposing theory to practice. It is also about having the experience of managing many similar conversations over the years and knowing that, for instance, in the above exchange, unless the therapist helps the mother reflect on her attitude to her daughter, the daughter will not alter her behaviour.

Thirdly, it is important that the therapist be 'present in the moment' (Rivett and Street 2001). Interest in this aspect of therapeutic presence has most recently entered family therapy practice via ideas about mindfulness that have come from cognitive behavioural therapy (Germer *et al.* 2005; Siegal 2007). However, many earlier therapists have suggested that the therapist needs to cultivate a state of mind in which external and internal experiences are being noted and a choice is made about which experience to privilege at any one moment within the therapy (Kopp 1977). One technique of mindfulness is that of the therapist bringing her concentration upon the minutiae of her own mental process. Becoming aware of these processes within the mind then becomes a powerful tool for the development of therapeutic presence in family therapy. Precisely because family sessions can be so busy explains why it becomes more crucial for the therapist to be aware of as many conscious and unconscious processes within themselves as the session progresses as possible. The purpose of such training is to help the therapist notice those 'intuitive' thoughts that are often lost.

There are a number of ways of teaching the therapist to be 'mindful' of her internal processes, many of which are based essentially on the meditative process. Kopp (1977), Welwood (2000) and Epstein (1996) recommend this form of mindfulness training for therapists.

76

Developing a therapeutic style

There are many dimensions that have been used by therapists to describe the factors involved in therapeutic style. Here we will consider two: the dimension of 'intervention style' and the dimension of 'relationship style'. To some degree family therapists possibly more than most therapists have a variety of styles that they can adopt. This is because within family therapy there are ranges of models that move from being very active in the therapy role to being quite passive and reflective. Traditionally, these differences have been characterised by the more reflective Milan style up to the more active and interventionist structural or strategic styles. In the development of a family therapist, the therapist needs to decide which place on this scale they feel most at ease with, but must also learn to adapt her style to the needs of the therapy session. It is important to establish that therapeutic style and therapeutic presence do not necessarily conflict with each other. Thus a therapist can have presence within any of the dimensions of style that we will discuss.

An interventive style, which is characterised by activity, could be observed in the following way:

- The therapist would move about during the session.
- She may involve family members in moving seats.
- She may move her own seat or even squat down next to a quiet family member to enable them to contribute.

There are many quite active techniques that such a therapist would adopt, for instance a family sculpt – asking family members to stand and position themselves in the room in accordance with how they feel about an issue. At times such active techniques might draw on wilderness activities (Plotkin 2003) or involve equine therapy, in other words taking the family therapy outside the therapy room itself. A more passive stance would be demonstrated by the therapist using questions and conversation to stimulate family change. Here the therapist would seem to invest more responsibility for change in the family system.

The 'relationship dimension' (Morgan and Sprenkle 2007) might be described as falling between two other extremes: collaboration and direction. Once more in the history of family therapy, these styles are represented by different models of therapy. Thus many of the early 'first order' therapies such as structural, strategic and possibly even Milan tended to be directive in terms of how they influenced family change. In these styles, the therapist needs to feel comfortable with making suggestions in a directive way and more willing to impose a direction on the session. Collaborative approaches on the other hand have been more represented within the third order post-modern approaches to family therapy (Anderson and Gehart 2007). Here, the therapist retains a curious and involved stance but allows the client to lead the therapy session rather than imposing a direction or purpose upon it.

Since family therapy has continued to hold a predominantly 'non-state' theory of the self (Rivett and Street 2003), it is evident that family therapy will also assume that at different times the therapist will adopt a varying number of styles within these dimensions. For instance, in the initial stages of therapy it is more appropriate to balance intervention with collaboration, whereas once the therapeutic alliance has been established the therapist might find it more appropriate to become more interventionist and directive. Equally, some types of family might prefer a more authoritative therapist than a collaborative one. Some problems might be best suited to a collaborative approach rather than a directive one. Within any particular family therapy session, the therapist might veer from one style to another. For instance, when strong emotional material arises, it is often more helpful for the therapist to be less directive and more reflective in order to help the material emerge in a safe way without the family members feeling criticised or not heard.

77

The use of disclosure in therapy

The discussion about styles of self in therapy connects to the use of revelation/disclosure of self in therapy. Once more we can see that the use of self-disclosure may be related to how colla- borative or active a therapist may be in their style. Shadley (2000) for instance found in her research that some therapists saw therapy as an 'intimate interaction' and therefore saw self-disclosure as crucial in helping to develop an honest, open relationship with family members. On the other hand, some therapists see this as inappropriate behaviour for the therapist and so limit self-disclosure to a minimum. Here they would disclose an aspect of themselves only if it was required within the particular context of the therapy session. Once more context may determine the comfort with which therapists approach self-disclosure. Lerner (1999) for instance describes working with a family in which the father had been diagnosed with cancer. He reports that within the therapy session he revealed that he, the therapist, was in remission from cancer. This was disclosed as a way of helping the family cope with the diagnosis. He states that this was helpful to the family even after the father had died. Roberts (2005) also writes very eloquently about talking with families about her own family struggles. However, the context for both of these writers is that they work in private practice within smallish towns in the USA. Family therapy practice in the UK differs significantly from this: In the UK the profes- sional role is much more pronounced within the NHS and families are less likely to already know the local 'therapist'.

In current reflecting team practice however, the disclosure of self has become slightly more common (Andersen 1991). In part this is due to a recognition that there is a crucial aspect of therapy that is *witnessing* the suffering of family members. White (1995) and Hoffman (2002) have talked about how this idea has taken root in their therapy and they have gradually encouraged team members to share their own personal struggles within the reflecting process, so that the clinical families can feel less alone in their problems. This remains quite contentious. Some therapists would only want to share their own lives if this did not increase feelings of failure for family members and if it did not detract from the predominant focus of the session, which is to help families (not therapists). What is interesting is that it is not always easy to know at the time of a disclosure whether it is 'too much', 'too critical' or 'too self-indulgent'. Accordingly, caution is probably the most appropriate approach in this area.

The wounded healer and human suffering

Many therapies recognise that there is something faintly odd about the profession of therapy. It appears to be an unusual and rather unnatural way to earn a living: to hear about the suffering and pain of others. Research into the stress levels of therapists, and particularly into the high cost of work with abused, violated and tortured individuals, shows that there is a human cost to being a therapist (Street and Rivett 1996; Varma 1997). In earlier points we have highlighted that many family therapists appear to be predisposed to family therapy from experiences within their own families. This would seem to be confirmed by the application that some have made of the concept of the 'wounded healer' to family therapy (Miller and Baldwin 2000).

This idea, originally a Jungian one, suggests that family therapists have some psychological experience or psychic trauma in their childhood or early adulthood that explains why they have chosen to train as family therapists. The assumption is that their experience will enable the healer to do two things. It will drive the healer to heal as a way of healing themselves and, paradoxically, it will help the healer stay in touch with the pain of suffering and not distance herself from pain so much that the client family will feel that there is no empathy/connection in the healing relationship. One possible implication of this 'wounded healer' theory is that the family therapist *has* to have encountered problems to 'make' a *good* family therapist. We suspect that most families who come for therapy would be quite disturbed to think that they are indirectly giving their therapist therapy and not the other way around. In other words, imagining the doing of therapy as therapy for the doer of therapy is quite outrageous. There does however seem to be an important message within the 'wounded healer' idea, which is that the therapist must have some connection to the suffering of human beings in order to truly help. This does not mean that a therapist needs to have experienced every problem presented to them during the course of their professional life, although in a career that spans 40 years this might be closer to the truth than not. But it is probably true that they have to have an understanding of psychological unhappiness, disease or distress in order to empathise or witness the pain of family members within the consulting room.

Thus therapists do need to have an understanding that they are also struggling individuals who continue to cope with challenges, relationship distress and pain during the course of their lives. It is possible that the function of compassion (Gilbert 2005) enables the therapist to feel this suffering and not be constrained therapeutically by it. This description is, of course, very far from the language of evidence-based practice and the 'scientific practitioner' description of clinical psychology, but it perhaps ensures that a humanistic perspective beats within the heart of family therapy.

It is also curious that large numbers of therapists report having a religious or spiritual understanding of their work (Rivett and Street 2001). The literature on family therapy and the use of spiritual resources is also large. This includes Christian, Buddhist, Islamic and Hindu (Bateson and Bateson 1988; Walsh 1999; Carlson and Erickson 2002; Kwee *et al.* 2006) perspectives. Again, it is not necessary for a family therapist to hold such views, but it demonstrates that for some family therapists the wounded healer concept has a more fundamental basis: that the source of the wound is as centred in a spiritual context as in a psychological one (Rivett and Street 2001).

Cultural competency and the family therapist

Systems theory would appear to make it obvious that different cultural systems will have an impact on what is relevant, what is acceptable and what is effective within family therapy. Yet, it was not until the 1980s that family therapists began to discuss these issues (McGoldrick *et al.* 1982). Initially, debates centred around the question of 'what did the therapist need to "know" when working with diverse groups?' This implied that a working knowledge of every culture that a therapist encountered was important (McGoldrick *et al.* 1996). Later, understandings about the nature of racism (sexism and hetero-sexism also) helped family therapists recognise that, despite the rhetoric of equality, social constructions of power meant that therapy with ethnic minority families had to be different from therapy with other families. In the 1990s, more and more analysis was undertaken to equip family therapists with both the theoretical and reflexive skills needed to work with families from diverse groupings such as minority ethnic families, gay and lesbian families and different cultural groups. This has given rise to the concept of 'cultural competency', which is now an essential element of family therapy practice. O'Hagan (2001) defines this as:

> . . . the ability to maximise sensitivity and minimise insensitivity in the service of culturally diverse communities. This requires knowledge, values and skills . . . the workers need not be . . . highly knowledgeable about the cultures of the people they serve, but they must approach culturally different people with openness and respect – a willingness to learn. Self-awareness is the most important component in the knowledge base of culturally competent practice.
>
> (2001: 235)

There are a number of aspects to cultural competency. One is the willingness to learn from families about what matters to them within their culture. This requires both humility and openness and the confidence to ask about such matters. For instance, a family that had fled violence in Africa told a family therapist that the community folk healers were the most important for healing their child, not therapy. In this case, the therapist needed to be respectful and interested in this description and not impose a western 'white' model on the family. Another 'skill' is to be able to gather helpful information about different cultural practices but being willing to recognise that the field is prone to racial and cultural stereotypes. An example of such a stereotype might be that 'black families have more community support than white families'. If the therapist was not able to challenge this (often) internal 'myth' she may fail to appreciate the lived reality for the family she sees and will destroy a good relationship with them (Burnham and Harris 2002). Thus knowledge (e.g. 'facts') might provide the general, but not the specific (Rivett and Street 2003).

The final aspect of cultural competency that has become significant for family therapists is to understand their own cultural, racial and sexual biases. If a therapist has not explored these, then they are likely to embody biases when working with diverse families. These biases may be conscious or unconscious. Clearly such biases will influence the curiosity of the therapist and limit how she can help the family. These biases can be opened up by having dialogues with colleagues as well as interrogating their own family cultural traditions. One technique developed within family therapy is for the therapist to draw up his or her family tree whilst noting cultural diversity. Hardy and Laszloffy (1995) suggest that different symbols might be used to mark which family members come from different cultural groups. Such an approach can apply to race, culture, class, language and sexual orientation: Cultural competency is not only about race and culture. This process will usually be undertaken in training or with a supervisor and its purpose is to help therapists understand how they might inadvertently make assumptions about diverse families and hence negatively influence the process of therapy. Because family therapy incorporates ideas about social power within its analysis, it is possible for family therapists to explore how different families experience them as therapists, be they white or from a minority ethnic group. There is now a body of literature designed to help all family therapists to address any racist assumptions in their practice (McGoldrick and Hardy 2008) and to use techniques from family therapy to explore such issues. O'Hagan (2001) comments that cultural competency is not only about self-awareness: it is also a therapeutic stance of openness and respect. It includes a willingness to learn about diverse cultures. It is therefore important that family therapists read widely and are exposed to diversity in their training. Some would describe this aspect of training as the most challenging.

80

Finding a place of 'not knowing'

We have characterised the fundamental therapeutic stance of family therapy as that of being curious. More recently, this stance has been varied by the description that the family therapist approaches her work from a position of 'not knowing'. There are various ways in which this concept or, more accurately, *therapeutic stance* can be understood. Using a metaphor from art, we might suggest that 'not knowing' is the state of consciousness when the methods of creation are so ingrained, so part of the artist, that they are no longer consciously drawn upon. A similar metaphor exists within the literature about Zen enlightenment. Here, it is suggested that the heart of enlightenment becomes part of the marrow in the centre of the bones rather than the skin of the practitioner (Reps 1971).

However, because the concept of 'not knowing' has created a certain amount of misunderstanding, Anderson (2007) has explained it in a more analytical way. She says that this stance includes four particular ideas:

1 The therapist must 'let go' of any preconceptions about the person they are working with. 'You must learn about the person from the person' (Anderson 2007: 49).
2 The therapist should retain a scepticism about her own therapeutic knowledge.
3 The therapist uses her knowledge as 'food for thought and dialogue [rather than being] authoritative, objective or instructive' (Anderson 2007: 49).
4 The therapist offers knowledge in a 'tentative and provisional manner' (Anderson 2007: 49).

For Anderson, 'not knowing' does not mean that the therapist knows nothing, or that the therapist never uses what she does know. Rather, it contributes to a stance of uncertainty that allows the therapist to fully listen to the family and enable their own solutions and reflections to emerge.

This therapeutic position might be understood as a position that therapists learn as they become more experienced and practised. It approximates to the free floating consciousness that a psychoanalyst would aim to achieve in the therapeutic space or the deep sense of experiencing the other of a Person Centred counsellor. Because it may be more possible for experienced therapists to enter this 'not knowing' place, it can be quite hard to see it as an approach that can be taught. This is why many of the family therapists who privilege 'not knowing' have written extensively about using collaborative methods in teaching therapy (McNamee 2007). Here the emphasis is upon creating a conversational space in which learning can occur as a parallel to the process of therapy where change can occur through the therapist's 'not knowing'.

In contemporary practice, many family therapists will see this newer idea as an extension of curiosity. Therapists will rarely impose a view of the family upon the family but would explore their own ideas tentatively and respectfully: '*I may be wrong here and I really want you to let me know about your ideas about this, but I have a hunch that there is a connection to you feeling that the world is unsafe and Jenny inviting anorexia into her life. Does that fit at all for you?*' At other times, the therapist will demonstrate reflection themselves in order to show that they don't 'know' what to say or do: '*Do you mind if I just think for a moment as I am really not sure what we should talk about next. Sometimes I am not quite sure what would be helpful . . . do you have any ideas?*' Always the therapist takes their own knowledge lightly as we have said. The initial meeting is always about how the family see things and what issues they want to use the family therapy to consider: '*Obviously, your doctor gave me some idea about what has brought you here, but it is more important that I hear your ideas. Who wants to help me understand what you think we can use these sessions to talk about?*'

Part 9

DEALING WITH COMMON CHALLENGES IN FAMILY THERAPY

81

How to manage 'resistance' in family therapy

Before we begin to consider ways of managing 'resistance', it is useful to reflect upon the meaning of the word itself (Anderson and Stewart 1983). Many practitioners would regard the concept of resistance as unhelpful, if not dangerous. Carpenter and Treacher (1989) for instance note that the term has often been applied to families but a truly systemic concept would include therapists and the agencies they work for as contributing to resistance. For instance, a therapist may say 'I do not work with these kinds of families' and not surprisingly receive 'resistance' back from those families. Equally, an agency might limit the kinds of problems they work with, so when a family outside this definition arrives the family will feel unwanted and therefore become uncooperative. Carpenter and Treacher (1989) also point out that certain families may be rejected unconsciously by the therapist themselves for reasons that have to do with their own family scripts. For instance, some male therapists will find dominant fathers in families difficult as this behaviour reminds them of their own experiences. As a result they will fail to listen to the father and undermine him non-verbally. Not surprisingly, that father will display behaviour that is increasingly dominant (to get himself heard) and will get labelled 'resistant' by the therapist.

More contemporary family therapists have sought to integrate one of Milton Erickson's ideas (de Shazer 1982), which was that the therapist should reframe resistance as a curious form of cooperation and *go along with it*. This approach encourages the family therapist to understand why a family or family member is *apparently* resisting therapy and see the roots of this in the behaviour of the therapist, not in the behaviour of the family member. Indeed de Shazer described 'resistance' as 'therapist's error'. The word meant to him that 'the therapist wasn't listening' (Hoyt 2001).

Given family therapy's preference for multiple perspectives, here we assume that something is happening in the relationship between family member, their context (including past experiences of help), the agency and the therapist that can be described as 'resistance' (a both/and perspective). There are a number of ways of 'interpreting' such interactions. Some situations can be understood in the terms we outlined in Point 36: That the family has an ideology of problems and problem solution that denies the usefulness of seeking therapeutic help. In other cases, especially where outside agencies are involved, the family may see the therapist as a pawn who is drafted in to make the family change to satisfy the outside agency (Turnell and Essex 2006). In the terminology of solution-focused therapy, individuals are either 'customers' (e.g. wanting therapy), 'complainants' (e.g. wanting to complain about others not taking responsibility for themselves) or 'window shoppers' (e.g. not really interested in therapy). The task of the therapist in these situations is to talk with family members to understand what they want out of therapy and explain what it can and cannot do. For instance, it is not uncommon for some families to see therapeutic services as a route out of cramped and unsatisfactory housing. Clearly, a family therapist should not embark upon a series of therapeutic sessions in this case but should clarify the family's needs and write in support of a house move!

Equally, if a family arrive for therapy and have a view that they have been 'made' to come by an outside agency, the first task of the therapist is to explain what can be done and how this might influence the way the agency deals with the family. Such careful contracting (Point 20) might take more than one session and might work best if a representative of the referring agency meets family and therapist to explain what they are wanting from the therapy. Usually, such an open and collaborative approach helps family members to see that the therapist is there to provide what will help the family resolve both internal and external problems. Resistance within a session will often be evident by either critical responses of the family or non-involvement. In the former case, the therapist should find a way of repairing the therapeutic alliance (Point 26) and spend time discussing what the problem is: '*I notice Jane, that every time I ask you to think about something, you tend to shrug your shoulders or say that wouldn't work. It is important if I am to help you that I understand what is going on here. Are my questions too complicated, are my suggestions silly or do you just not think I can help anyway?'* Hopefully, such honesty will stimulate a conversation that will lead to more involvement in the therapy.

Family members who have little to say are another example of 'resistance' in the therapy room. There are a number of ways of encouraging contributions in this situation. One is to find alternative ways of communicating: Perhaps language is too difficult for some family members. This might be an invitation for the therapist to adopt a more active and playful stance that encourages involvement. Alternatively, it might be too much 'problem' talk that family members find difficult. This can often be the case when adolescents do not take part in sessions: It feels too painful and they feel either blamed or feel that their parents are being blamed. A simple remedy is to limit the problem talk and agree to talk about something the teenager wants to talk about first. One of our frequent techniques is to invite youngsters to bring music into the session that has a particular meaning for the young person. This then becomes the theme of the conversation and has the added advantage of reframing the typical adult view that teenagers' music is 'just noise' with the implication that it has meaning for the teenager.

82

How to manage getting 'stuck' in therapy

Feeling 'stuck' is a common experience for most therapists and usually happens after the therapy has been progressing for a number of sessions. It is hard to clearly define what is meant by 'being stuck' but usually it involves a lack of progress in treatment outcomes and a feeling of malaise within family and therapist. Beaudoin (2008) defines stuckness as: 'an absence of movement or as movement towards an unhelpful direction' (2008: 78).

Family therapists approach this process in a number of ways. The most obvious way is to 'return to the start' and renegotiate the targets of therapy with the family. This action ensures that the therapist is working on the same target as the family: a mismatch will inevitably result in these stuck feelings.

Sometimes, the therapist has to acknowledge with the family that they appear to have stalled in their work together and try to have a conversation that checks if the therapist knows everything that he or she needs to know. For instance, if there are secrets or significant events that the therapist does not know about, the lack of attention to these might be relevant to the stuckness in the therapeutic system. This conversation might centre around the question: '*Have I missed anything significant? Is there anything that might have a bearing on our situation that you have not told me?*' This conversation clearly needs to be a non-blaming one in which the therapist takes responsibility for part of the working difficulties and does not criticise the family for what is happening in the therapy process. However, the therapist should also notice if she feels that 'the therapist is working too hard'. This particular process suggests that the family is not taking responsibility for changing their own lives and are assuming that the therapist will do this. This might have multiple causes, one of which might be because they do not think they can do anything and feel powerless in the face of the pressures on them. Another common experience for therapists is to find that the family are continuing using the therapy sessions to talk about 'yet another crisis' without being able to move on to tackle the problems that underlie them, e.g. their coping style.

In both of these examples the therapist must work hard to understand the feelings evoked in the therapy room and to make conscious the beliefs that might underpin them.

The phrase 'therapeutic system' demonstrates one of the crucial approaches to this issue that family therapists bring: they consider the role of the therapist, the therapist's context *as well as* the family in the creation of a stalled process. An issue in any one of these might lead to halted progress in treatment. For instance, the lack of progress might be because the therapist has lost a sense of optimism in the treatment. This in turn might be because she has failed to overcome the same kind of problem in her own life. Rober (1999) has argued that stuckness in the therapy process is often the result not of factors within the family but because the therapist has lost either her sense of optimism or courage! Beaudoin (2008) also comments that stuckness commonly occurs when therapists become too centred upon the problem and lose their *systemic perspective*.

There is one other technique that family therapists routinely use when faced with stuckness: they invite different family members into the therapy. The reason for doing this is because some important family member, who has not been part of the therapy, might be 'holding' it up. By bringing them in, they can join the process and hopefully help rather than hinder. This might be evoked by asking '*Is there anyone else we should invite into our sessions who can help us move on from this stuck feeling?*'

When family therapists are stuck with cases, like most other therapies, they will take the case to supervision (Elizur 1990). However, they might also ask a team to join them with the case or ask another team member to join them for consultation with the case. These additions make it less likely that the stuckness will persist. In a supervisory setting, the therapist will be encouraged to think about what has been missed, about how they interact with the family and what different therapeutic options they could adopt to resolve the delay in progress.

83

How to manage conflict within a session

Given that many families come to family therapy with hidden conflict and major unhappiness, it is not unusual for a session to erupt into a conflict. Once more the personal style of the therapist is important here. Some therapists are more comfortable and able to manage conflict than others. If conflict erupts, it is quite likely to be the moment when the therapist feels most inadequate! Many will have assumed that the best way of managing conflict is to reflect upon it: '*I wonder if this kind of row happens at home a lot of the time?*' Sometimes of course such an intervention may only fan the flames and contribute to the escalation of the conflict, with the father saying: '*Of course it does and I often end up having to stop her from going out with her friends.*'

In these situations, the therapist has to gauge how useful it is to pursue this theme. For instance, if the therapist feels that violence could break out in the session (and this may be information gained from intuition as much as from the family), then it would be wise to stop the conjoint session and review how therapy can be helpful (e.g. making a 'no violence' pact or seeing family members separately). However, if the family want to resolve their conflicts without such heat *and* the therapist feels able to help, then there are other techniques that can be used to deal with the conflict. One is to seek agreement to investigate the emotional roots of the conflict, which usually will be to do with feeling unloved or not listened to: '*I can see that you get very worked up about this issue. What do you think the anger is trying to say?*' Here circular and reflexive questions can invite family members to see their conflict within the terms of their relationship and can help them take responsibility for how they respond, rather than falling back on blaming: '*How does blaming him for your anger help you either get him to do what you want or make you feel better about life?*'

There are more radical options that again can be traced to other systemic techniques. For instance, the therapist might reframe the conflict: '*It is good that you are able to express yourselves and to know that you love each other so much that this will not affect your deep feelings for each other.*' Or a positive connotation might be used by emphasising the intent of the conflict: '*I know that you are choosing to show anger because there is something you really want your family to hear: what might that be?*' If the therapist has worked with the family for a while, humour might be a valuable tool: '*Is this a private row or can anyone join in?*'

The main tool for the family therapist when conflict emerges is to retain a sense of *themselves as a therapist* and not be scared of what comes out: it is after all part of the process of therapy.

84

How to manage strong emotions in a session

It might be thought that because family therapy is predominantly concerned with patterns of relationship, it rarely 'delves' into the realm of strong emotions. By this we mean not the angry ones discussed above but ones of sadness, loss, depression or self-loathing. This would be incorrect because family therapy, like all other therapies, opens up a space for family members to speak in ways and about things that they wouldn't do at home. It is true that in family therapy the therapist will always be seeking to connect these feelings to other family members. The therapist will also be asking how deep feelings in one family member affect other family members. But such strong emotions are voiced and always should be attended to.

The father of one girl cried at the end of the first family session because for the first time in years he connected his feelings of sadness for his daughter with his feelings of loss for his mother who died five years before. When family members are distressed in this way, the family therapist asks other family members to comfort the person: '*Tell me Jim, who should comfort you now?*' Then as the pain of the memory recedes, or the rawness of the feeling slackens, the therapist will explore the relational aspects of the experience.

Therapist:	Jim, why did thinking about your experience with your mother bring up your experience with your daughter?
Jim:	At the end of her life I feel I let my Mum down, now I feel I let my daughter down.
Therapist:	Do you think other family members know about this aspect of how you think?
Jim:	No I keep that private: I have to be strong to help them get through.

> *Therapist*: (*To wife*) Did you know he was harbouring all this since his mother died?

In this example, the therapist did not ignore the strong pain of the father, but tried to bring the feeling into a relational pattern as soon as possible. This would be the same approach if a family member talked about feeling depressed.

> *Therapist*: Julie, you describe how you feel with the word 'depressed', I wonder if you think any other family member has got experience of depression?
>
> *Julie*: Yes, my Mum and her Mum have said they get depressed. But that is different from mine. They have never tried to kill themselves.
>
> *Therapist*: Are you sure? Have you ever asked them? You know they might have some tricks they know to fight depression if they have experienced it.
>
> *Julie*: (*To mother*) Have you Mum?
>
> *Mother*: (*To Julie*) Yes I have but you have to get on with it don't you?
>
> *Therapist*: Julie, can you hear what your mother is saying – she has a way of managing those feelings?
>
> *Julie*: No. I think she is saying I am weak and stupid for giving in.
>
> *Therapist*: That's interesting, so the depression has got between your relationship and made it hard to hear when your Mum has ideas that could help you.

On another occasion, the therapist might try to help Julie and her Mum work out how different and similar their experiences of depression were so that they are more able to recognise their own needs and resources.

In all such situations, the family therapist must assess the risk of the situation and if necessary ask for support with the case from the wider professional group, such as GPs and psychiatrists.

85

How to manage secrets and half truths

Because they work with family groups, family therapists frequently find themselves in possession of a number of family secrets. Examples of this would be where perhaps the referrer mentions that the father of a child is not the man living with the child (and the child doesn't know), or perhaps that one family member has had an affair and the partner doesn't know. Such secrets can come out in a number of ways. As described, referrers might let the therapist know, or a family member may contact the therapist and tell him/her, or a secret may come out unexpectedly whilst the family therapist draws a family tree. It is best in the latter case to warn the family not to disclose secrets before drawing the family tree.

Family therapists have a number of approaches to 'holding secrets'. On the whole, the view is that being in possession of a secret constrains therapy and forces the therapist to be dishonest to the person who does not know. Therefore, most therapists would wish to meet with the secret 'holders' and discuss how to proceed. Carpenter and Treacher (1989) comment that such a process is an integral part of the therapy in that it establishes an agenda in which the secret becomes something to talk around and place within an interactional setting. For instance in the case of an affair the therapist might ask: '*Who would be most hurt by revealing the secret and how might you reveal it in a way that lessens this pain?*' Indeed, sometimes the secret can be externalised and discussed as an influence upon the family:

> If something had happened to your daughter, who would be most able to manage it? How might this help the family discover some new ways of coping and some resilience? How might you as a family work together on helping your daughter get strong again? What would be the worst thing that could have happened and what makes it the worst?

In the above example, where we are assuming a child has been sexually assaulted but is too afraid to tell, the therapist is effectively painting in the background (Jones 2007) of the secret rather than actually talking about it. This technique has similarities to Erickson's use of hypnosis in which he asserted he could work with a problem without knowing anything about what it was (Erickson and Rossi 1981).

Unfortunately, there may be occasional situations in which the therapist does have to hold a secret *in the interests of one family member*. An example of this might be the case suggested above: A GP refers a child and his family to family therapy and mentions that it is a secret that the man whom the child calls 'father' is not actually his father. The therapist might in this situation meet the parents first to decide how significant this fact was in the problems that the family were managing. If it was not significant and the parents barred the therapist from telling the child, then it is conceivable that the secret would be kept. On the other hand it is quite likely that the secret somehow informs relational patterns in the home and may be one of those secrets that everybody, including the children, knows about but they do not acknowledge it. In such a situation, the therapist may want to talk about how to talk about the secret.

How to manage absence from sessions

In terms of family therapy, rather than making the heart grow fonder, absence is a great loss. In family therapy, for a family member to be absent is a form of communication (we have already noted that all behaviour is a form of communication). Even worse, it might be a form of disqualification of the therapy itself. Some family therapists have seen the absent member as a potential 'enemy' of therapy and have argued that they may undermine therapy from afar and therefore the therapist must make efforts to contain them within the therapeutic process. The Milan team managed this by refusing to see a family unless all the relevant members were there (Palazzoli *et al.* 1978). Skynner (1976) on the other hand tried to understand which family members were crucial for change to occur and would ensure that they came to therapy.

There are a number of strategies that can be used to try to involve absent members. One strand is to entice the absent family member to come to therapy. This can centre upon sending messages via the family members who do come, or alternatively writing to the family member to help explain why their views are so important.

Typically, separated fathers are both 'forgotten about' by helping agencies and also tend to absent themselves because they either don't wish to get involved or are critical of the care their child is being given by their ex-partner. In such situations, it is often the case that the dynamic of separation is contributing to the way the family help their child grow up and so it is import- ant to involve the father. Here a letter such as the following might be helpful:

Dear x,
As you know your son is having a few problems and we are trying to help him overcome these. We know he sees

you as a very important person in his life and we are sure that you have ideas about how to help him. We would therefore like to meet you to hear your ideas and perhaps arrange for you and your son to meet us together

Often this helps the father see the value of meeting with the therapy team. If a family member has been to therapy and then refuses to come back, the therapist may also write to them and seek to entice them back by referring to what was said and sometimes to what was said about them.

Of course sometimes a family member suffers from a disability and cannot attend. This is particularly true when working with three-generational families where there are elderly grandparents. In such circumstances, the therapist may think it appropriate to visit the family home to work with the whole family at least once.

87

How to manage children who 'misbehave' in sessions

There are various approaches to managing this situation and some of them come from the strategic school of family therapy (Point 62). One such approach would be to congratulate the child for showing his or her difficulties in the session. Clearly, such behaviour is an invitation for the therapist to explore how different or similar what is being shown is to what happens at home. The therapist also ought to be able to find a way of talking to the child about its behaviour so that the child feels included in the discussion. Systemically, the therapist might ask the child's parents how they handle this kind of behaviour and might even invite them to do what they would normally do at home: '*I notice that Gemma is playing on her own as we talk here and she is getting more and more angry about something. When she throws things around like this at home what do you do?. . . . Could you try that now to see if you can help Gemma get more in control of herself please?*'

How the parents complete or try to complete this task will provide valuable information about how such situations are managed and with appropriate feedback to the parents inter-active gains can be made. This activity will occur if a particular issue is the behavioural management of children, however since systems theory assumes that all behaviour is a form of com-munication, angry or disruptive behaviour can also be inter-preted as a message: '*I wonder if Gemma is asking us to talk more about this or less about this?*' Of course in any intervention the therapist should seek to have the parents bring the child along with the process. Sometimes, the therapist can de-escalate children's behaviour by asking for cooperation from the child and accepting their own limitations: '*You know Gemma, I am just so slow I can't think when there is so much noise in the room. Could you help me a little by turning it down a bit please?*'

However, whatever happens in these situation the therapist continually needs to allow the parents to feel that ultimately they have responsibility for the child: '*What was it that I did then that resulted in Gemma becoming quiet? Did I deal with her in the best way?*'

There are finally two considerations to keep in mind. Sometimes, children's distress and hence misbehaviour in a session can be because they are communicating something that is either secret or cannot be turned into words. The therapist should be alive to this as a possibility and address it in whatever way necessary. Sometimes this will involve assessing the risk to the child in the family and may require a referral to a child protection agency. Moreover, the therapist should be careful not to appear to condone any abusive forms of control that may represent punitive child-rearing practices. Lastly, sometimes the therapy might be more successful with parents alone rather than having the child present and further allowing the child to undermine the parents in a conjoint session. The aim in such a separated intervention would be to help them gain more control of their child's intense emotions. Team work (Point 98) provides family therapists with many other options: A team member might play with the child within a family therapy session, or may work with the child in another room while the family work continued.

88

How to manage failure

In a sense 'failure' is a very unsystemic concept (Coleman 1985; Carr 1990). If systems theory states that all systems change over time and that it is difficult to predict how change will occur or to which place it will lead, it is probably inappropriate to ascribe 'failure' to any therapeutic intervention. However, the reality is that therapists will do so: they will 'punctuate' change such that they cannot see any result from their interventions. Managing 'failure' is therefore a crucial aspect of both managing the self and the role of the therapist. The literature confirms that work-related stress and what has been called 'burnout' are often connected to feeling overresponsible for change and this is connected in turn to feeling that too often one fails to help families (Varma 1997). In some contexts this experience can be very common. For instance, some difficulties carry with them less hope for change and more chronic presentations. Many family therapists will moreover be asked to see families who have been offered treatment by other professionals, perhaps over years, and in whose family dynamics 'problems' seem to multiply. In such situations, it is important that the therapist retains a clear view that he or she is a facilitator for change but not the sole guardian of it: the family, the context and other agencies often also have a responsibility here. Therapists must also recognise their own capacities and humanness: they are not able to 'cure' all human suffering and indeed some would argue that such an approach contradicts the basic human condition (Gehart and McCollum 2007).

The other important aspect of failure is to learn from it. There are many books and papers that help therapists to 'reframe' failure as a learning process (Kopp 1976). In other words, failure is part of the process. Many family therapists will report learning crucial themes from understanding why they have 'failed'. Family therapists, because they value openness in their therapeutic work, will often talk with families about their failures – sometimes with the family itself and sometimes with later families: '*I do not appear to have been able to help here. Do you have any ideas for me in future about what I might have done differently?*'

The other learning aspect of failure is that the therapist will recognise the high value to good supervision, good personal support systems and good institutional processes. The former (supervision) is where therapists explore what may have not worked well and learn from it. The second aspect (personal support) helps therapists put their work into perspective: Although therapy is in many ways a vocation, it is also 'just' a way of earning a living. In terms of this issue, therapists will oscillate in their investment in their work depending on their own stage of family life cycle development. For instance, a therapist with no family commitments may have more investment in their work and therefore be more prone to being affected by failure. Whereas a new parent who is also a therapist may be less affected. Of course, in supervision the relationship between these 'life spaces' and the occurrence of failure will be explored.

Helpful institutional processes are also crucial in helping therapists to understand failure. Haley (1981) originally warned family therapists that most mental health institutions were unlikely to be supportive to a family systems approach. Surveys of family therapy practice (Street and Rivett 1996) have confirmed that the most stressful aspect of family therapy work is often the institutional setting. However, agencies can be helpful to therapists when failure occurs. For instance, they might support referral on to other agencies. They might also support therapists if the failure has led to the family wishing to complain about the therapy. Complaints procedures are now part of professional registration and being the subject of a complaint can be extremely distressing for therapists. Such a process changes the confidential 'learning from failures' into a public accusation of incompetence. It is even more important at these moments for family therapists to have strong support systems in place.

In a survey, Street and Rivett (1996) explored what kinds of support systems family therapists use. The methods most often quoted were team support, supervision, personal therapy and collective spiritual practices. This work highlights that family therapists must, like all other workers, maintain a healthy work/ life balance with particular reference (as they are family therapists) to contexts and systems.

Part 10

FAMILY THERAPY IN CONTEXTS

89

General contexts of practice

There are a number of 'general contexts' in which systemic and family therapy skills are used (Treacher and Carpenter 1984; Street and Dryden 1988; Carpenter and Treacher 1993). Professionals using these skills are not necessarily all labelled as family therapists, although in the UK the title will shortly be subject to statutory regulation. Indeed, many professionals who have been trained in family therapy would use these skills within the normal routine professional tasks that they undertake. Thus it is quite likely that a social worker, a mental health nurse or a psychologist will employ family therapy skills whilst working *as* a social worker, nurse or psychologist. However, within certain contexts there will also be a small number of family therapists who have trained to qualifying level and are employed as family therapists. In different countries family therapists are found practising in different settings that to a large extent are determined by how that country has constructed their health and social welfare institutions. In the UK family therapists are most frequently found in child and adolescent mental health settings (CAMHS) and adult mental health, whilst in the USA family systems ideas are employed within medical settings more commonly than elsewhere and, of course, in private practice.

Unlike many other therapies, family therapy has an intimate relationship with its contexts of practice. Of course, this relationship is not without its tensions. Within the UK at least, both CAMHS and adult mental health work come within the ambit of the National Health Service (NHS). This institution has an overarching medical ideology, so family therapy has sometimes had to struggle to assert its broader systemic approach. This is clearly the case in both CAMHS and adult mental health, where the prevailing modality of treatment can become diagnostic (which labels individuals, presumes a certainty of the problem and lacks curiosity) and centres upon medication (not psychotherapy;

Rogers and Pilgrim 2001). Nevertheless, family therapy within these contexts remains particularly vibrant and most of the practice literature has evolved from these settings (Carpenter and Treacher 1993). The flourishing of family therapy in these contexts is connected to its ability to adapt within contexts, not unlike the way Buddhism adapted as it spread across the silk route (Williams 2009). This means that the form of family therapy in each context might vary. Within CAMHS and adult mental health, family therapy can be characterised as integrative, problem focused and accountable (Rivett 2008). Usually, family therapy is requested in these settings by a member of the multidisciplinary team. Indeed, this team member may continue to have a role in managing the case (e.g. providing medication, support or individual work with the referred individual), therefore the family therapy undertaken will integrate various approaches (as described in this book) and respect the perspectives of other team members (Speed 2004). The family therapy will normally be problem focused and will employ family systems techniques in order to improve the referred 'problem behaviour/relationship'. Lastly, family therapy within these contexts has developed a strong research and efficacy base in order to justify its practice (Sprenkle 2002; Sexton et al. 2003; Carr 2009a, 2009b).

There are a number of growth areas within the practice of family therapy and systemic practice in particular contexts. In adult mental health practice, Seikkula (2002) has developed the use of systemic crisis meetings when a person is experiencing a psychotic episode. In the treatment of 'anti-social' young people, Henggeler (Sheidow et al. 2003) has developed a form of multisystemic therapy that also contains a strong systemic approach to difficulties. Both of these approaches have a developing evidence base. The recent years have also seen a growth in the use of family therapy within a multi-family group intervention. Such groups have now been trialled in eating disorders, depression and early psychosis (Eisler 2005). Again these groups demonstrate an integrated model of family therapy that also incorporates techniques from other therapies, such as motivational interviewing (Steinglas 2009) and psycho-educational ideas.

90

Contexts where abuse has occurred

Family therapists have been very active in areas where abuse has occurred and something of the originality of the field shines through in these situations. It is very easy in situations of abuse to adopt a simple approach that castigates the abuser and sees its role as the ending of abuse. From a therapeutic perspective, however, such action is only the start of the healing process. For instance where a child has been sexually abused, a therapeutic approach would seek to heal the relationship with the main carer and help the child process the abuse such that it has minimal influence on the child's later life and development. Family therapy contributes to this therapeutic approach in a number of ways. Firstly, family therapy would want to work with the carer and child together at least for some of the time, as family therapy would argue that relationships are best healed *in vivo*. Secondly, family therapy, with its ability and preference to hold a number of different perspectives, would be able to work with the complexity and ambivalence involved in this healing. Thus feelings of anger, resentment and rejection can be heard as well as those of caring, love and guilt. In other words, family therapy would not assume that healing between mother and child would be easy, as each have lost something of their lives in the process of abuse and disclosure. Lastly, family therapy would ideally wish to ensure that there is a process of reparation that occurs between abused and abuser, with the expectation that such work would free the child to manage future relationships with the abuser and others. In practice this latter process rarely happens.

In the UK a large number of family therapists undertake this work as court experts, as CAMHS professionals or as specialists working in social service settings. There are a number of significant characteristics to how family therapists approach this work. One is that family therapists are able to manage 'uncertainty' within the context of abuse. An example of this is the work of Turnell and Essex (2006), who have developed a way of working in child abuse situations where no clear 'abuser' has been identified (or acknowledged). Such situations are quite common. This method of working is called the 'Resolutions Approach'. Drawing upon solution-focused and narrative ideas, it creates a collaborative relationship with parents or carers that has as its focus *'how can we work together to make sure your child is protected'*. Using a number of creative techniques, including co-constructed stories, the Resolutions team help the family plan appropriate child protection irrespective of who has been alleged to have caused the original abuse.

Another characteristic of work in contexts where abuse has occurred is that of family therapists' ability to manage complexity and multiple descriptions. This is nowhere truer than in the field of domestic violence. Therapy within this domain of practice is a disputed subject (Rivett 2006) and it is important to remember that the priority in any context of abuse is the safety of individuals. Thus, family therapists will assess for safety and risk before embarking upon couples or family work where domestic violence has happened (Goldner 1998). However, given the large incidence of abusive relationships (Home Office 2000) and the variety of presentations by the members of these relationships, family therapy can be helpful.

Goldner *et al.* (1990) explained that because family therapy is able to recognise multiple descriptions of events, it is well suited to working in the complexity of 'volatile relationships'. These authors propose that by accepting that some couples want to continue their relationship but want the abuse to stop, family therapists can intervene by using a variety of theories to explain their techniques. Goldner *et al.* (1990) believe that systems theory can help to explain how an abusive pattern builds up in the relationship; feminism can explain why men feel entitled to treat their female partners abusively (and why women feel trapped in such relationships); and psychodynamic theory can explain how the couple attachment dynamic works. The therapeutic intervention therefore relies on challenging the abuse, empowering the woman and unpicking the emotional features of the 'attachment'. Often, this therapy centres around the violent or abusive incident in order to deconstruct these factors.

Therapist:	So when you say your wife broke your hand what do you mean?
Male client:	Well I went to punch her and she shut the door on my hand.
Therapist:	OK so let's look at that again, who broke your hand and what do you think your wife would say about that?

Within the UK, Goldner's ideas have been adopted by a number of services, most notably those established by Cooper and Vetere (2005). In these examples, the therapy has a focus on healing the mother–child relationship before attending to the rehabilitation of the couple relationship. Cooper and Vetere (2005) also are insistent that their form of therapy is only safe in domestic violence if a third party agency, such as social services or probation, acts as a monitor of safety and compliance. Although family therapy and therapeutic perspectives in general are less prevalent than other approaches (Rivett and Rees 2004; Rivett 2006; Rivett *et al.* 2006) in domestic violence services, there is increasing acknowledgement that criminal justice responses are insufficient and a wider systemic approach has much to offer (Rivett and Rees 2008).

91

Couples' and marital therapy

Although traditionally couples' therapy has attracted many behavioural and psychodynamic interventions (Gurman 2008), family therapy and systemic ideas are increasingly prevalent in the work. It is equally true that the contexts in which family therapists work, even if they are not normally labelled as couple therapy ones, will frequently require attention to the couple or parenting relationship. For instance, when one partner has a diagnosis of depression, there is strong evidence (Jones and Asen 2000) that work with the couple can improve the depression. This would therefore be a role for a family therapist working in an adult mental health context. Within services for children and adolescents, systems theory would assume that the couple relationship will impact upon the parenting relationship, therefore again a family therapist may need to attend to this more intimate work.

In couples' therapy, systems theory and family therapy provide a way of connecting past with current patterns of relationship, gender roles with social expectations of these roles and behaviours with meanings. Because of its strong 'here and now' emphasis, many versions of couple therapy that are informed by family therapy tend to emphasise interactional patterns between partners rather than unconscious processes. A recent example of this is the work of Gottman (1999; Gottman and Gottman 2008). In a series of experimental studies, Gottman isolated patterns of interaction that he hypothesises have a relationship to later separation. In particular, Gottman noted that when couples criticise each other frequently, when there is a defensiveness, when men show contempt for their female partners and when each partner 'stone walls' (does not respond to) the other, they are less likely to stay in the relationship. These four behaviours Gottman called the *Four Horsemen of the Apocalypse*. In his studies, Gottman was able to predict with remarkable accuracy which couples would separate a number of years later depending upon their score in these behaviours. This 'empirically based theory' (2002: 167) led Gottman to design a form of couples' therapy that teaches couples to listen to each other, construct positive interactions, create shared life dreams and value each other.

An alternative, also evidenced based, systemically informed couples' therapy is that of *emotion-focused couples' therapy* (Johnson 2003, 2008). This model of couples' therapy, once more, concentrates upon the interaction of the couple within the therapy room. Johnson (2003) draws on attachment theory to understand why unhappy couples behave the way they do and she aims to help them practice new ways of relating within the therapy hour, so that they can transform their relationship at home. Emotion-focused couples' therapy has explored *what the therapist has to do to help couples change*. This form of research is called *process research*. Johnson has isolated one particular aspect of this process, which she has called *the blame-softener process*. This describes the process by which the therapist hears one partner blame another for his or her behaviour and then explores the intention of that blamed partner with the blamer. This process usually leads to the blamer understanding the emotions behind the action and this 'softens' the blame.

Therapist:	When he says he can't be with you as he has to work, what happens for you?
Female partner:	I get angry and feel rejected.
Therapist:	So you interpret his actions as meaning he does not care about you? What does that sound like for you? (*to male partner*).

This elicits a recognition from both partners that they are locked in misunderstandings and the apportioning of blame: their problem is an interactional cycle, not each other.

Therapist:	You both seem very sad that you have got into this way of being with each other. Can you see each other's pain?

Male client:	Yes I just buried the feelings I felt about our relationship, and I only saw her as having a go at me. I didn't understand how alone she felt.
Female client:	It is good to hear you talk like this. I just never thought you were bothered about how I felt.
Therapist:	What do you think it has been like for him?
Female client:	I think he has felt alone too. All these years both of us alone!

Within the domain of couples' therapy, one area in which family therapy can also provide a significant contribution is where one partner has had an affair (Coop Gordon *et al.* 2008). Affairs and the discovery of them frequently take couples into therapy. A family therapist working with a couple where one partner has had an affair will consider the affair within the context of each partner's own meanings and family scripts, within the context of the current relationship and within the context of a 'process' in which a couple may or may not choose to repair the relationship damage of the affair. A family therapist will also work with the systemic consequences of the affair, e.g. with in-laws and with children. There has been an extended discussion within this field of the relational meaning of forgiveness (Walrond-Skinner 1998). This discussion has proposed that forgiveness is not a quality of an individual but is more a quality of a relational pattern between individuals.

92

Consultation and family therapy

Family therapists have a long history of applying their modality to organisational consultation (Wynne *et al.* 1986; Campbell *et al.* 1989; Pratt *et al.* 2005). This is largely because ideas about how families work as systems can easily be transposed to how organisations work as systems. The range of contexts in which family therapists consult to organisations is vast. For instance, on a clinical level, a family therapist may need to consult to a school about how to work with a child or family. Such a clinical situation can easily evoke interventions about how the school manages situations such as bullying, which might have broader impacts on the school ethos or hierarchy. Family therapists have also applied their systemic skills in work with statutory agencies, private businesses and family businesses (Wynne *et al.* 1986). In such consultations, family therapists bring with them ideas about patterned habitual behaviour, understandings about the role of leadership and ideas about how beliefs and cultural assumptions constrain behaviour.

Often, just as in families, the difficulties in the system may be put down to blaming one or other teams or groups within the organisation. In such consultations there is often a presumption that the consultant will 'fix' the 'problem team/group' so that the organisation can continue to flourish. The consultant responds in exactly the same way as a therapist does with a family: explores the resources of the organisation, provides a space where difference can be discussed and seeks to open up communication. Seeing the organisation as a system means that the consultant looks for transitions that are often the harbingers of change and disruption. For instance, many family businesses reach a transition when the entrepreneurs who founded them retire. The organisational culture that served them well during the early development of the businesses and often relied on strong, committed leadership has to change. This can be a fraught period for the business and many 'first generation' family businesses do not manage to last into the second generation. A systemic consultant would be aware of these developmental issues, which are present in different forms in all organisations. The intervention therefore is like that with families: helping the organisation change its hierarchy, culture and beliefs to manage the change more smoothly. Some systemic consultants emphasise the beliefs of the individuals within the organisation, rather than the structure of the organisation:

> Over time, patterns of working behaviour become established so that workers can observe that 'this is the way we do things here'; the organisation is no longer an abstract set of structures, but in people's minds becomes a living organism that has a culture and that powerfully affects – and is affected by – individuals' values, beliefs and behaviour.
>
> (Campbell 1999: 45)

Recent work by Campbell (Campbell and Groenbaek 2006) takes the interest in meanings within an organisation further. He now works by unpacking the 'polarities' of thinking within an organisation. For instance, within one service, there may be differences between those who think that 'everyone should share the same skills' and others who think that 'each person should specialise in one skill'. Campbell suggests that without this polarity neither view has a meaning, in other words the two views are a system and rely on each other. Therefore, in his consultations he helps to uncover why certain individuals hold to one set of views rather than another and how they would alter the way they behave within the organisation if they chose an alternative view. This process leads into a constructed conversation between individuals who hold different views so that their conflict or competition with each other can be moderated. This systemic method of organisational consultation is designed to 'unstick' unhelpful conflict between teams, groups and hierarchies.

Some of the ideas and techniques used in the field of organisational consultation have themselves flowed back into the practice of family therapy. One such example is that of appreciative inquiry (Hammond 2006). Appreciative inquiry incorporates many of the assumptions of systems theory and family therapy. For instance, there is a presumption of competence ('what works well') and questions are seen as a primary way of creating change. The interventions with organisations focus on issues such as 'how to be proud of the organisation', or 'what dreams and aspirations' of the organisation do individuals have. This positive, appreciative process then leads to the construction of a proposition for the improvement of the organisation.

93

Private practice

Many family therapists work in private practice, which holds its own unique contextual challenges. The first of these is the relationship between the therapist and the referrer: Most families find a private practitioner through another professional, whether it be a GP (Dimmock 1993) or another psychological therapist. This relationship may affect the types of families that the therapist meets and determines the relationship between therapist and referrer (e.g. does the therapist inform the referrer about progress?). For instance, if a psychiatrist referred a family to the family therapist, it might be assumed that issues of mental health will have been addressed and hence family members are able to take a full part in the therapy. On the other hand, if another therapist has referred the family, questions about risk and safety may need to be assessed before work was undertaken. This is one of the essential differences between private practice and agency-based family therapy – in the latter there is usually a multi-disciplinary team who can help the therapist assess risk collaboratively, whilst in private practice this resource is not available. This leads to private practitioners being perhaps more careful about the families they work with. It also means that the practitioner needs to maintain relationships with referrers so that appropriate and safe referrals are made.

Because family therapists hold a systemic framework, they would be aware that often the referrer of a family has himself become 'part' of the family system (Palazzoli *et al.* 1980b). Thus a private practitioner would need to understand what role the referrer has with the family and make sure that this dynamic is attended to.

A child and his mother were referred by his aunt to a private family therapist. This aunt had a professional position within a helping system and was paying for the treatment of her nephew and her sister who was a lone parent on low income. As the therapist talked with the mother and son, he discovered that this aunt was seen as a disciplinary parental figure by the boy and was seen as a critical influence by the mother. The family therapist therefore had to talk with the aunt about her role in the family and her expectation of the therapy before continuing treatment.

It is also important for the therapist to find a way of reflecting upon the position that the family are expecting the therapist to take. In the above example, the mother might have wanted the therapist to 'change' her son. In a private context this might make initial discussions of treatment targets even more crucial. Many family therapists undertake court assessments and this might lead them to give evidence in court, which might lead to disagreements between various 'sides'. Again, in such circumstances it is important that the therapist receives clear instructions about what is required of the party that employs her.

The other significant issue for family therapists in private practice is that of ensuring that they receive appropriate supervision and support. Both of these are requirements for the professional registration of therapists. The former is usually provided by another systemic or family therapist. There is a presumption that therapists are supervised by colleagues from within their own modality, although sometimes therapists chose to experience difference in their supervision (Street and Rivett 1996). Again, because family therapists are aware of the context of their work, it is important that such supervision attends to aspects of practice that might be challenging. It is possible that in a situation in which private therapist pays private therapist for supervision, a collusive relationship pattern might be created.

There are also major practical challenges to private practitioners: they must be able to manage the business side of their work and be able to feel comfortable in charging for their trade. This itself can raise many issues about family tradition, political allegiance and competitiveness.

94

Diversity

In this book we have emphasised the importance of diversity for family therapy practice (see Points 14, 15, 16 and 79). All the contexts in which family therapists work will entail diversity and the issues that it raises. In Part 8 we highlighted the importance of cultural competency for family therapists. It is however also important that family therapists are aware of issues of diversity within all aspects of the everyday practice of therapy. Diversity is *not only* an issue about practice with minority ethnic families, it is ubiquitous. Family therapists should be careful in assuming that they share beliefs about families, beliefs about values and beliefs about appropriate behaviour with the families they are working with. This is where curiosity and the respectful use of questions becomes a technology for understanding and exploring diversity. It is also important that therapists are open to be changed themselves by the news they receive. Burnham (1993) has talked about the social GRRAACCES as an aide to recognising the variety of issues of diversity within clinical practice: gender, race, religion, age, ability, class, culture, ethnicity and sexuality. Burnham's acronym begins with the phrase 'social' because, as systemic therapists, family therapists are aware of the influence of social constructs upon the individual. Hence, the concepts of power and oppression are vital in understanding how some of the issues of diversity are experienced (McGoldrick and Hardy 2008).

For instance, a white family might experience discrimination and bullying because they have come to the UK from Eastern Europe. A black family may experience similar discrimination but, because of the history of racist ideologies and of institutional racism, their experience may be qualitatively different and more distressing. In the therapy, these differences will need to be explored in order to orientate the therapist about the context of problems. But also, by exploring these issues trauma and pain may be put into words in such a way that the family may be able to gain more control of their lives or alter their relationship to the trauma. Sometimes, for relatively privileged therapists to hear about the racism, bullying and abuse that occur in the UK can be shocking. This feeling cannot be allowed to limit the capacity to listen and help families in such situations.

Working with diversity has therefore a number of elements to it. The therapist must be able to be open and respect difference but it is also about making sure that the therapist is orientated to some of the lived experience of diverse families, such as knowing something about families who hold firm religious beliefs (Walsh 1999; Carlson and Erickson 2002), the process of coming out for gay people within a heterosexist society, the experience of physically handicapped parents or the struggles of lone parent families. This experience can be learnt in a number of ways, not all of which have a clinical component. For instance, it is valuable for therapists to gain experience in working in various settings such as community projects, disability projects or specialist services for minority groups. It is also useful to learn how to talk about diversity in friendship groups in ways in which the therapist's experience is enriched. In most training settings, family therapists are encouraged to 'interview' non-clinical families and learn how child rearing, couple relationships and 'family' are viewed. Clearly any particular therapist cannot know everything about all these diverse family systems. However, it is also common within family therapy for therapists to use 'cultural consultants' to deepen their understanding of diverse families and to work hard in learning how to use interpreters in their work (Raval 1996).

Throughout this book we have woven the technology of family therapy with both the self of the therapist and the theory of systemic therapy. This 'three-armed' trident is equally relevant in diversity practice. The family therapist needs to be equipped with a working knowledge of diversity issues, needs to manage her curiosity to avoid assumptions (e.g. 'not knowing') and needs to rigorously enquire about her own cultural 'blocks', which in this context are often experienced as certainties. These certainties need to be explored and challenged, as they are frequently childhood/family biases and scripts that introduce 'otherness' into diversity practice and therefore compromise the curiosity and respect needed.

Part 11

DEBATES AND ISSUES

95

Integrating other therapeutic modalities into family therapy

When family therapy first emerged in the 1960s it sought, quite vociferously, to assert its own superiority over other extant forms of therapy. Thus Haley (1981) and others criticised 'insight'-based therapies and therapies that expected the therapeutic relationship to achieve results alone (person-centred therapies). During the life cycle of family therapy, this tradition of isolationism has continued with almost an obsession, with the latest philosophical trend and attention given to exotic practices within family therapy rather than to the developing world of other therapeutic modalities.

As always, such a version of history privileges one story rather than any other. For instance, we could equally note that Robin Skynner (1976), a pioneer of British family therapy, incorporated psychodynamic ideas into the field. Moreover person-centred ideas have also been important (Street 1994). However, this period of insularity certainly began to be eroded in the 1990s and has reached a fruition of sorts in the 2000s. Now, more and more family therapists have brought ideas and practices into the field that originated in other therapeutic traditions. For instance, the use of psychodynamic ideas has mushroomed, with a number of authors asserting that family therapy can learn both from the insights of intra-psychic processes but also from the emergent object relations schools (Flaskas and Perlesz 1996; Flaskas *et al.* 2005; Pocock 2005, 2006). Where family therapists are working with substance misuse they are importing motivational interviewing techniques into their family sessions (Miller and Rollnick 2002; Steinglas 2009). Whilst the influence of attachment research has also had effects in terms of family therapy practice (Hughes 2007), we might also argue that postmodern ideas have encouraged the field to go 'full circle' and 're-invent' person-centred ideas within a collaborative and constructionist paradigm (Anderson 2001).

An interesting development in terms of the integration of concepts from other areas of study has been the adoption of psychobiological insights by family therapists. This began with studies by attachment researchers on how secure attachments contributed to the growth of the infant brain. This has now become more general, with practitioners sometimes using psychobiological ideas in their couple and family work. Fishbane (2007) for instance explains to families that when they react negatively to each other this is because their amygdale (a 'primitive' part of the brain) is wired to react this way. She explains that therapy seeks to increase the ability of the neocortex (the 'social' part of the brain) to contain the primitive urges of the amygdale.

The reasons for family therapy's more open approach to other theories may be both developmental and contextual. Some authors have suggested that family therapy is now an established form of therapy and no longer needs to be either 'insecure' or 'dismissive of alternatives' (Rivett and Street 2003). There is also an argument that says that all ideas and practices, including therapeutic modalities, undergo a certain development that begins with isolation and moves to assimilation with the dominant culture. Additionally there are also contextual, pragmatic reasons why family therapy has had to 'adapt' and integrate other therapeutic ideas. Firstly, clinical reality rarely replicates the 'textbook' case examples, so family therapists may find that they need to draw on a wider theoretical base than the one predominant within their field. Secondly, most family therapists come to family therapy via a previous training. These trainings, such as social work, nursing, clinical and counselling psychology and medicine, will often have their own therapeutic theory that will continue to influence family therapists no matter what their 'new' training encourages. Lastly, most family therapy posts exist within multi-disciplinary teams in which psychiatrists, nurses and psychotherapists of varying modalities will also work (Speed 2004). In such a context, a merging of approaches is both likely and also essential if team collaboration is to be maintained rather than inter-professional rivalry. Family therapy therefore has become more of a mature and possibly less challenging therapy during this developmental process.

96

Family therapy, family support and family counselling

Walker and Akister (2004) comment that 'while few practitioners are employed as family therapists, a great many in family support roles will be using similar techniques and strategies'. This begs the question: 'How do we define what we have been talking about in this book from other forms of "family intervention"?.' This becomes even more complex when research guidelines are considered that frequently talk about 'family work' and rarely specify 'family therapy' or 'family counselling' (NICE 2004a, 2004b, 2004c, 2004d, 2005, 2006). The easiest way of answering this question is to assume that the activity undertaken by family therapists is family therapy and that undertaken by others is a variant of family work. Unfortunately, this is not a very helpful answer. As noted previously, many other professionals are also trained, at least to a degree, in family therapy. Walker and Akister (2004) suggest that there is a hierarchical distinction to draw: Family support tends 'to be marginalised as an activity without [a] clear definition' and they argue that as such it is a 'poor relation' in comparison to family therapy. It is certainly true that on some levels this marginalisation appears to be changing. UK governmental guidance is currently suggesting that all professionals should 'think family', with 'family support' seen as an important intervention to avoid poor outcomes for children, higher academic achievements for boys and greater social inclusion.

Hardiker (1995) has provided possibly the most inclusive way of thinking about the way family services are structured. She defines 'family support' as having three levels. At the primary level are the universal services designed to strengthen family functioning. In the UK such services would be health visiting, family income support as well as universal school provision of the nature of after school clubs, etc. At the secondary level are the services designed to improve the outcomes for specific groups of families, usually those seen as at risk of social exclusion. Services such as Sure Start in the UK and other 'targeted' services come under this heading, as do those such as mediation services. The last level (tertiary) of family support is where specific problems have arisen, such as mental illness, abuse, domestic violence and where intensive work needs to be undertaken to prevent further difficulties.

In this categorisation, family therapy would seem to be a subclass of family support and predominantly focused on the tertiary level. However, clearly many family therapists also see families at the primary and secondary level, especially if they are in private practice. It would seem that this definition helps but is not quite adequate. We would propose that family support is any activity that gets alongside families and supports them in their everyday activities. This support becomes therapeutic when emotional and psychological problems are addressed. Usually the family support worker will draw on counselling theory in an attempt to alleviate these problems. In this role there is an assumption that the helping relationship and the act of listening will be enough to make a difference. *Family counselling* (O'Leary 1999) is therefore a description of family work based on person-centred ideas. However, a family support worker might draw on family therapy as well as counselling ideas during the work with a particular family.

As mentioned, *family work* is also a frequently used term. A number of NICE (2004a, 2004b, 2004c, 2004d) guidelines, for instance, mention this activity as being indicated as a treatment option. *Family-based interventions* and *family-focused treatment* are two other similar phrases. Often these terms refer to psycho-educational as well as the more traditional family therapy approaches. We should therefore assume that all these terms fit onto a continuum, at one end of which there is some involvement of family members in the construction and implementation of a treatment plan, but this is not necessarily *conjoint or systemic*, and at the other end is conjoint systemic family therapy (as described in this book).

97

What is postmodernism and why has it influenced family therapy so much?

Postmodernism has been defined in a number of ways but it is best to see it as a critique of *modernism*. Modernism is described as the idea that society and knowledge form a progression from a less advanced state to a more advanced state. Therefore modernism would be the philosophy that sees that humanity is 'progressing' and that the ideals of liberal, democratic societies are becoming universal. From a scientific position, modernism is the idea that knowledge grows and gradually we know more about more things. In contradiction to this, *postmodernism* is a philosophical and cultural view that asserts that there are no 'universal truths', no 'deeper' structures to uncover and no progression to a better society (Lyotard 1984; Lyon 1994). Postmodernism has been summarised as a concern for the local, a rejection of the grand narratives of social movements/knowledge and respect for the marginalised. Key writers within postmodernism are Foucault, Derrida (Loewenthal and Snell 2003) and Gergen (1999, 2008), Gergen being a particularly important theorist for family therapists.

It is not surprising that family therapists became excited by postmodern ideas. Family therapy has a tradition of seeking exotic and challenging philosophical ideas on which to base its practice. In the 1970s something similar happened when family therapists adopted second order cybernetics (the view that the observer was part of the observed). Postmodernism, with its scepticism of truth, its assertion that social discourses create meanings and its thorough going belief that the self was a social construct (Gergen 1999, 2008), fitted with many of the early systemic ideas. Furthermore, postmodernism seemed to justify difference and uncertainty. Therefore, in the 1980s and 1990s when postmodern ideas fully filtered into family therapy, it created a revolution in the thinking of many family therapists.

At the same time many family therapists seemed to have lost their allegiance to systems theory for many of the reasons mentioned in Part 2, so the arrival of a different metaphor for practice was immensely appealing. The consequence of this was that family therapists began to regard systems theory as a modernist grand narrative itself and instead adopted narrative models for therapy, such as those of Michael White and David Epston (1990).

There can be no doubt that this movement was helpful to the field of family therapy. It continues to act as a corrective to a mechanical reliance on systems theory and it has given family therapy some important new techniques and ways of seeing problems in families (McNamee and Gergen 1992; Freedman and Combs 1996; Freeman *et al.* 1997). Many of these have been part of the fabric of this book and continue to be integrated into the practice of most family therapists even if they do not call themselves 'narrative therapists'.

There are well described critiques of the narrative developments in therapy (Flaskas 2002; Rivett and Street 2003). There are however two practical consequences of the rise of narrative within family therapy that are important. The first is that narrative therapy is now almost divorced from family therapy altogether. Many contemporary narrative therapists do not know how to interview families, they do not know how to use the aliveness of conjoint family interventions and they do not work with interactions in the way family therapists do (Minuchin 1998). This trend away from family therapy has mirrored a similar development in the field of solution-focused therapy. Secondly, the integration of narrative within family therapy has shown that a field that has often been bedazzled by new ideas has become more likely to adapt and adopt rather than transform. This is a crucial ability when a therapy has to prove its efficacy in the evidenced-based world of contemporary practice.

Teams and co-therapy in family therapy practice

The use of teams in family therapy was one of the fundamental discoveries of the approach. Although teams were used before and co-therapy was common as a practice, it was the Milan school of family therapy that described them as an 'indispensable tool' for family therapists. The original authors (Palazzoli *et al.* 1978) argued that the team structure allowed the therapist to enter the family's reality whilst relying on the team he or she was working with to escape becoming as 'stuck' as the family. Further, the team structure, whether the family was interviewed by one or two colleagues, made concrete the view that in each system there would be many interpretations and many perspectives. It was the 'job' of the team to represent these interpretations and perspectives.

The Milan team established the classic way that family therapy teams work. A family therapy session was divided into five sections. In the first section, the team would meet before the family arrived to discuss hypotheses that could orientate the therapist when the family was seen. The second section consisted of the therapist interviewing the family in front of a one-way mirror using the hypotheses discussed within the team. The third stage consisted of the therapist leaving the family alone and in private and talking to his or her team about which hypotheses seemed useful and what kind of intervention might be helpful. Usually, the intervention was constructed between the team and the therapist and was often written down. In the fourth stage, the therapist returned to the family and gave the family a message from the team. And lastly, after the family had left, the team reconvened to review the session and their ideas about how the intervention worked or would work and whether they had revised their hypotheses.

In time, a number of critiques of this model emerged. It was said that this way of working encouraged the presumption that the 'team knew best' and that the one-way mirror was used to privilege the team's perspective. Indeed, one commentator saw the mirror as equivalent to the surveillance used in prisons (Epstein 1993). With the influence of postmodernism, there clearly was no going back to what was interpreted as an inappropriate, dominating, expert-led form of therapy. However, Andersen (1991) suggested that there was a way of using teams and screens in a more collaborative manner. He instituted a way in which the team became much more involved in the therapy and shared their ideas with the family rather than keeping them within the professional system. This model was called 'the reflecting team' model because the team reflected about what they had been thinking in front of the family and therapist rather than the therapist joining the team in private. This turned the private therapy sphere into a public process. Sometimes, the team simply reversed the screen technology so that the family and therapist could see into the room behind the one-way screen and hear what the team had to say. Inevitably, as team members shared their ideas, they also found that they disclosed more about themselves and they felt accountable for what they said and how they said it. The result was a gentle, thought-provoking conversation in which team members are positive about the family members' intentions and offer different perspectives on solutions, experiences and processes.

However, few practices in family therapy stay still. Narrative therapy practitioners took the reflecting team even further. White (1995) implemented a procedure in which the reflecting team became a 'witnessing' process. This then became an opportunity for the family to hear outsiders witness the struggles they either had or were going through. This was intended to free them up to find new ways of resolving difficulties. A variation on these uses of teams is now very common in family therapy practice.

Many observers who think of family therapy automatically think that it always involves teams. Indeed, some criticise it for such an expensive use of professional time. It is therefore significant that most family therapists do not spend most of their clinical time in such teams. Indeed, many do not have the 'luxury' of such teams. In most statutory agencies, family therapists might spend half a day per week working in a team. These team clinics would be reserved for the most complex cases (such as child abuse, severe mental health problems) and also those cases that individual family therapists needed help with (e.g. they were 'stuck'). In such situations, it is probably true that teamwork allows the therapist to work with very complex situations and it also protects the productivity and efficacy of the therapist, who is less likely to be 'burnt out' (Street and Rivett 1996).

99

Training and supervision in family therapy

In the UK, The Association for Family Therapy and Systemic Practice (www.aft.org.uk) regulates and accredits the training of family therapists. It specifies the standards of training and then becomes a route for the registration of family therapists. To qualify as a family therapist, the student has to have a set amount of live supervised practice as the primary therapist during the course of her course. This means that the student is supervised by a supervisor (a qualified family therapist and usually a registered supervisor) in their face to face work with families and usually this will be via the one-way screen. This model of training has been a hallmark of family therapy since its origins. Family therapy early on rejected the idea that supervision could be adequately done via case discussion. Just as the emphasis in early family therapy was on changing patterns *in the room*, so the training of family therapists has emphasised changing therapeutic practice *in the room*. It is traditional for a student's work to be videotaped so that the tapes can be reviewed to find significant alternative interventions and interactions. In live supervision, the supervisor can phone through to the student and suggest some alternative questions or interventions.

Family therapists bring to the supervisory task the same systemic perspective they bring to their work with families. Within systemic therapy this is a multi-layered process that applies to the supervision of students as well as clinicians. The therapist is seen as embedded within a number of systems, all of which may have an impact on the therapy offered to families. Lee and Everett (2004) talk about systemic supervision being an embedded process in which the supervisor holds in mind the various contexts of the therapist as well as the impact of the supervisory relationship itself. Thus in the supervision of any particular case, the supervisor will be alert to the family of origin dynamics of the therapist, to the way the dynamics in the family have an impact on the therapist and to the way the dynamics between supervisor and supervisee have an impact on the work. Within these levels, there will be gender issues, age issues and agency issues.

A therapist presented a case to her supervisor (a man) about a family whose adolescent daughter seemed to be acting out for no apparent reason. The therapist presented the case by saying 'some cases baffle us; this is one'. She had adopted a similar stance with the family. As the supervisor asked a few more questions, what emerged was that there were two daughters in this family, both of whom had different fathers. This was a secret and as such the eldest daughter's father had never been mentioned. Gradually, connections began to be made in the therapist's mind: she was a single parent who easily neglected to think about absent fathers; the secrecy in the family meant a crucial part of family history could not be discussed and this had evoked collusion in the therapeutic system. Perhaps the girl's behaviour was not so baffling.

Early family therapists largely adopted similar perspectives on supervision and training as they did in their clinical work. Thus Bowen (Haley and Hoffman 1967) argued that to be trained as a family therapist the supervisor must help the trainee separate from their own family of origin. Others argued that what mattered in family therapy training was learning the techniques not attending to emotional issues (Haley 1981). More recently, just as in therapy family therapists have begun to work with the therapeutic alliance (Point 26), supervisors are working with a 'common factor' (Morgan and Sprenkle 2007) approach to supervision. Here the task of supervision is understood as a combination of three dimensions: the nature of the relationship in the supervision (on a continuum of collaborative to directive); the emphasis of the task (from clinical competency to professional competency); and the specific issue being supervised (from particular case-based to general agency-based issues). This way of viewing family therapy supervision allows the supervisor to move from 'coach' in case supervision, to 'mentor' in respect of the professional role of the supervisee, to 'teacher' when it comes to talking about general case/agency issues and finally to administrator when it comes to the bureaucratic learning of the students. This is indeed an all-inclusive model for supervision that relates to other therapy models (Hawkins and Shohet 2000; Scaife 2001).

100

Towards the future for family therapy

This book has demonstrated that family therapy is a multi-faceted therapy that has undergone significant changes during the course of its development. Historically, it has gone through periods of intense change. In its early days the fervour of its pioneers seemed to promise interpersonal cures for many difficulties. During its more reflective days, it consorted with an array of philosophical ideas. Indeed McNamee has called it 'promiscuous' (2004). Some of its postmodern proponents would regard it as out of date and in Derrida's phrase 'erased' already! So in the early part of the twenty-first century what remains and what is family therapy's future?

This book has demonstrated the large body of techniques and theories that family therapy has created. Upon the bedrock of the 'metaphor' of systems theory, family therapy has created an interactive, interpersonal and vibrant therapy. There are signs that the interpersonal approach has itself begun to be accepted within other therapies and in particular the contribution of family therapy to evidence-based practice is growing. There are now a number of guidelines that recommend family therapy with certain psychological difficulties (NICE 2004a, 2004b, 2004c, 2005, 2006). Research about the efficacy of family therapy continues to grow (Sprenkle 2000; Sexton *et al.* 2003; Carr 2009a, 2009b). This research provides evidence that family therapy should be a requirement within child and adolescent mental health services, within substance misuse services, within adult mental health settings and within many medical settings. It has demonstrated the role of family therapy in work with socially challenging youth and in services to families who foster abused children.

There are a number of features that this increasing evidence base has highlighted (Rivett 2008). The first is that family therapy is usually *part* of the interventions for the situations outlined above. In other words, it is rarely the *only* therapeutic intervention. Thus the early claim that family therapy alone could offer cures for many problems has been softened. For instance, in work with socially challenging youth, family therapy will be one intervention amongst others that help young people to discover more helpful peer relationships as well as to address family poverty. In some situations such as work with depression and ADHD, family therapy is suggested as an intervention alongside medication. The second feature of this evidence is that family therapy is often distinct because of its interpersonal focus, which despite lip service is actually rarely present in other interventions. Thirdly, the model of family therapy practised is an integrated one, very similar to the model described in this book. It is rare that any family therapist still practises as a 'pure' 'Milan' or 'Structural' family therapist. Even the contemporary 'narrative' therapists incorporate ideas from other schools of family therapy (Lebow 2005). Lastly, again represented in these 100 points, is that family therapy has now incorporated techniques and ideas from other therapies to enhance its interpersonal focus (Rivett 2008). Family therapists therefore will use psychodynamic ideas, motivational interviewing practices and narrative techniques even though these are distinct therapy models in their own right.

Family therapy as a professional pursuit has gradually gained a foothold in many health and social care institutions in the last two decades. This seems likely to continue, both with the policy emphasis on family interventions and on the impending statutory regulation of psychotherapy. However, this process has led to a mainly female, well educated group of professionals who hold 'family therapy posts' (Rivett and Street 2003). At times during this professionalisation, it has looked as if the radical impulse of family therapy has waned. Yet this book has shown that in many fields family therapy continues to offer a coherent theory and a set of interpersonal techniques that can be transforming for families and their networks. The rich tapestry of techniques and ideas that have made up family therapy has also continued to make for a vitality and a verve. As a result, family therapy continues to apply its ideas to new settings. Family therapists are working in schools to prevent bullying, they are working in poor districts to help empower families and they are applying Buddhist mindfulness techniques with their clients (Gehart and McCollum 2007). Innovation has always been part of family therapy and this clearly goes on. This book is evidence that the core skills of family therapy and the core philosophy at its centre – that human beings are, by their very nature, interactional and have an embedded self within relationships – surely have a lot to offer the future of social policy and therapy in general.

References

Andersen, T. (1991) *The reflecting team: dialogues and dialogues about the dialogues*. New York: Norton.

Anderson, C. and Stewart, S. (1983) *Mastering resistance*. New York: Guilford Press.

Anderson, H. (2001) Postmodern collaborative and person-centred therapies: What would Carl Rogers say? *Journal of Family Therapy*, 23: 339–360.

Anderson, H. (2007) The heart and spirit of collaborative therapy: The philosophical stance – 'a way of being' in relationship and conversation. In Anderson, H. and Gehart, D. (Eds) *Collaborative therapy*. New York: Routledge, pp. 43–59.

Anderson, H. and Goolishian, H. (1988) Human systems as linguistic systems. *Family Process*, 27: 371–393.

Anderson, H. and Gehart, D. (2007) *Collaborative therapy*. New York: Routledge.

Bagarozzi, D. and Anderson, S. (1989) *Personal, marital and family myths*. New York: Norton.

Baldwin, M. (2000) *The use of self in therapy*. New York: Haworth Press.

Bateson, G. (1972) *Steps to an ecology of mind*. New York: Ballantine.

Bateson, G. (1979) *Mind and nature*. New York: Dutton.

Bateson, G. and Bateson, M.C. (1988) *Angels fear: Towards an epistemology of the sacred*. New York: Bantam Books.

Beaudoin, M.-N. (2008) Therapeutic movement and stuckness in family therapy. *Journal of Systemic Therapies*, 27: 76–91.

Becvar, D. and Becvar, R. (1999) *Systems theory and family therapy*. Lanham, MD: University Press of America.

Bogdan, J. (1984) Family organisation as an ecology of ideas: An alternative to the reification of family systems. *Family Process*, 23: 375–388.

Boscolo, L. and Bertrando, P. (1993) *The times of time: A new perspective in systemic therapy and consultation*. New York: Norton.

Boyd-Franklin, N. (2003) *Black families in therapy*, 2nd edn. New York: Guilford Press.

Bowen, M. (1972) Towards the differentiation of a self in one's own family of origin. In Framo, J. (Ed.) *Family interaction: A dialogue between family researchers and family therapists*. New York: Springer, pp. 111–173.

Brown, J. (1997) Circular questioning: An introductory guide. *Australian and New Zealand Journal of Family Therapy*, 18: 109–114.

Burbach, F. and Stanbridge, R. (1998) A family intervention in psychosis service integrating the systemic and family management approaches. *Journal of Family Therapy*, 20: 311–325.

Burbach, F. and Stanbridge, R. (2006) Somerset's family interventions in psychosis service: An update. *Journal of Family Therapy*, 28: 39–57.

Burnham, J. (1993) Systemic supervision. The evolution of reflexivity in the context of the supervisory relationship. *Human Systems*, 4: 349–381.

Burnham, J. and Harris, Q. (2002) Emerging ethnicity: A tale of 3 cultures. In Dwivedi, K. (Ed.) *Meeting the needs of ethnic minority children*. London: Jessica Kingsley Publishers, pp. 170–199.

Byng-Hall, J. (1995) *Rewriting family scripts*. New York: Guilford Press.

Campbell, D. (1999) Connecting personal experience to the primary task: A model for consulting to organisations. In Cooklin, A. (Ed.) *Changing organisations*. London: Karnac, pp. 43–62.

Campbell, D. and Groenbaek, M. (2006) *Taking positions in the organisation*. London: Karnac.

Campbell, D., Draper, R. and Huffington, C. (1989) *A systemic approach to consultation*. London: Karnac.

Carlson, T. and Erickson, M. (2002) *Spirituality and family therapy*. New York: Haworth Press.

Carpenter, J. (1987) Some reflections of the state of family therapy in the UK. *Journal of Family Therapy*, 9: 217–229.

Carpenter, J. and Treacher, A. (1989) *Problems and solutions in marital and family therapy*. Oxford: Blackwell.

Carpenter, J. and Treacher, A. (1993) *Using family therapy in the 90s*. Oxford: Blackwell.

Carr, A. (1990) Failure in family therapy: A catalogue of engagement mistakes. *Journal of Family Therapy*, 12: 371–386.

Carr, A. (2000) Family therapy: Concepts, process and practice. Chichester: John Wiley & Sons.

Carr, A. (2009a) The effectiveness of family therapy and systemic interventions for child-focused problems. *Journal of Family Therapy*, 31: 3–46.

Carr, A. (2009b) The effectiveness of family therapy and systemic interventions for adult-focused problems. *Journal of Family Therapy*, 31: 46–75.

Carter, B. and McGoldrick, M. (1989) *The changing family life cycle*, 2nd edn. Boston, MA: Allyn and Bacon.

Carter, B. and McGoldrick, M. (1999) *The expanded family life cycle*. Boston, MA: Allyn and Bacon.

Cecchin, G. (1987) Hypothesizing, circularity and neutrality revisited: An invitation to curiosity. *Family Process*, 26: 405–413.

Cecchin, G. and Lane, G. (1991) *Irreverence: A strategy for therapist survival*. London: Karnac.

Coleman, S. (1985) *Failures in family therapy*. New York: Guilford Press.

Coop Gordon, K., Baucom, D., Snyder, D. and Dixon, L. (2008) Couple therapy and the treatment of affairs. In Gurman, A. (Ed.) *Clinical handbook of couple therapy*. New York: Guilford Press, pp. 429–458.

Cooper, J. and Vetere, A. (2005) *Domestic violence and family safety*. London: Whurr.

Dallos, R. (1991) *Family beliefs systems: Therapy and change*. Milton Keynes: Open University Press.

Dallos, R. (1997) *Interacting stories: Narratives, family beliefs and therapy*. London: Karnac.

Dallos, R. (2004) Attachment narrative therapy: Integrating ideas from narrative and attachment theory in systemic therapy with eating disorders. *Journal of Family Therapy*, 26: 40–65.

Dallos, R. (2006) *Attachment narrative therapy*. Maidenhead: Open University Press.

Dallos, R. and Urry, A. (1999) Abandoning our parents and grand-parents: Does social constructionism mean the end of systemic family therapy? *Journal of Family Therapy*, 21: 161–186.

Dallos, R. and Draper, R. (2005) *An introduction to family therapy: Systemic theory and practice*. Maidenhead: Open University Press.

Dell, P. (1989) Violence and the systemic view: The problem of power. *Family Process*, 28: 1–14.

De Shazer, S. (1982) *Patterns of brief family therapy*. New York: Guilford Press.

De Shazer, S. (1985) *Keys to solution in brief therapy*. New York: Norton.

De Shazer, S. (1988) *Clues: Investigating solutions in brief therapy*. New York: Norton.

Dienhart, A. (2001) Engaging men in family therapy. *Journal of Family Therapy*, 23: 21–45.

Dimmock, B. (1993) Developing family counselling in general practice.

In Carpenter, J. and Treacher, A. (Eds) *Using family therapy in the 90s*. Oxford: Blackwell, pp 163–184.

Eisler, I. (2005) The empirical and theoretical base of family therapy and multiple family day therapy for adolescent anorexia nervosa. *Journal of Family Therapy*, 27: 104–131.

Elizur, J. (1990) 'Stuckness' in live supervision: Expanding the therapist's style. *Journal of Family Therapy*, 12: 267–280.

Epstein, E. (1993) From irreverent to irrelevance: The growing disjuncture of family therapy theories from social realities. *Journal of Systemic Therapies*, 12: 15–27.

Epstein, M. (1996) *Thoughts without a thinker*. London: Duckworth.

Erickson, M., Rossi, E. and Rossi, S. (1976) *Hypnotic realities*. New York: Irvington.

Erickson, M. and Rossi, E. (1981) *Experiencing hypnosis*. New York: Irvington.

Fadden, G. (1998) Research update: Psychoeducational family interventions. *Journal of Family Therapy*, 20: 293–309.

Featherstone, B., Rivett, M. and Scourfield, J. (2007) *Working with men in health and social care*. London: Sage.

Fisch, R. (2004) So what have you done lately? MRI brief therapy. *Journal of Systemic Therapies*, 23: 4–10.

Fisch, R., Weakland, J. and Segal, L. (1982) *The tactics of change: Doing therapy briefly*. San Francisco, CA: Jossey-Bass.

Fishbane, M. (2007) Wired to connect: Neuroscience, relationships, and therapy. *Family Process*, 46: 395–412.

Flaskas, C. (2002) *Family therapy beyond postmodernism*. Hove: Brunner-Routledge.

Flaskas, C. and Perlesz, A. (1996) *The therapeutic relationship in systemic therapy*. London: Karnac.

Flaskas, C., Mason, B. and Perlesz, A. (2005) *The space between*. London: Karnac.

Fredman, G. (1997) *Deathtalk: Conversations with children and families*. London: Karnac.

Freedman, J. and Combs, G. (1996) *Narrative therapy*. New York: Norton.

Freeman, J., Epston, D. and Lobovits, D. (1997) *Playful approaches to serious problems*. New York: Norton.

Friedlander, M. (1998) Family therapy research. In Nichols, M. and Schwartz, R. (Eds) *Family therapy: Concepts and methods*. New York: Allyn and Bacon.

Friedlander, M., Wildman, J., Heatherington, L. and Skowron, E. (1994) What we do and don't know about the process of family therapy. *Journal of Family Psychology*, 8: 390–416.

Friedlander, M., Escudero, V. and Heatherington, L. (2006) *Therapeutic alliances in couple and family therapy*. Washington, DC: American Psychological Association, pp. 503–533.

Gehart, D. and McCollum, E. (2007) Engaging suffering: Towards a mindful re-visioning of family therapy practice. *Journal of Marital and Family Therapy*, 33: 214–226.

Gergen, K. (1999) *An invitation to social constructionism*. London: Sage.

Gergen, K. (2008) Therapeutic challenges of multi-being. *Journal of Family Therapy*, 30: 335–350.

Germer, C., Siegal, R. and Fulton, P. (2005) *Mindfulness and psychotherapy*. New York: Guilford Press.

Gilbert, P. (2005) *Compassion*. London: Routledge.

Glick, I., Berman, E., Clarkin, J. and Rait, D. (2000) *Marital and family therapy*. Washington, DC: American Psychiatric Press.

Goldenberg, I. and Goldenberg, H. (2000) *Family therapy: An overview*. Belmont, NY: Brooks/Cole Thomson Learning.

Goldner, V. (1991) Generation and gender. In McGoldrick, M., Anderson, C. and Walsh, F. (Eds) *Women in families: A framework for family therapy*. New York: Norton, pp. 42–60.

Goldner, V. (1998) The treatment of violence and victimization in intimate relationships. *Family Process*, 37: 263–286.

Goldner, V., Penn, P., Sheinberg, M. and Walker, G. (1990) Love and violence: Gender paradoxes in volatile relationships. *Family Process*, 29: 343–364.

Gorell Barmes, G. (1998) *Family therapy in changing times*. Basingstoke: Macmillan Press.

Gottman, J. (1999) *The marriage clinic*. New York: Norton.

Gottman, J. and Gottman, J. (2008) Gottman method couple therapy. In Gurman, A. (Ed.) *Clinical handbook of couple therapy*. New York: Guilford Press, pp. 138–166.

Gurman, A. (2008) *Clinical handbook of couple therapy*. New York: Guilford Press.

Gurman, A.S., Kniskern, D.P. and Pinsof, W.M. (1986) Research on marital and family therapies. In Garfield, S.L. and Bergen, A.E. (Eds) *Handbook of psychotherapy and behavior change* (3rd edn). New York: John Wiley & Sons, pp. 565–624.

Haber, R. and Hawley, L. (2004) Family of origin as a supervisory consultative resource. *Family Process*, 43: 373–390.

Haley, J. (1973) *Uncommon therapy. The psychiatric techniques of Milton H. Erickson*. New York: Norton.

Haley, J. (1976) *Problem solving therapy*. San Francisco, CA: Jossey Bass.

Haley, J. (1980) *Leaving home: The therapy of disturbed young people*. New York: McGraw-Hill.

Haley. J. (1981) *Reflections on therapy and other essays*. Washington, DC: Family Therapy Institute of Washington Press.

Haley, J. and Hoffman, L. (1967) *Techniques of family therapy*. New York: Basic Books.

Hammond, S. A. (2006) *The thin book of appreciative inquiry*. Bend, OR: Thin Book Publishing Co.

Hardiker, P. (1995) *The social policy contexts of services to prevent unstable family life*. York: Joseph Rowntree Foundation.

Hardy, K. and Laszloffy, T. (1995) The cultural genogram: Key to training culturally competent family therapists. *Journal of Marital and Family Therapy*, 21: 227–237.

Hawkins, P. and Shohet, R. (2000) *Supervision in the helping professions*. Milton Keynes: Open University Press.

Hildebrand, J. (1998) *Bridging the gap*. London: Karnac.

Hoffman, L. (1993) *Exchanging voices*. London: Karnac.

Hoffman, L. (2002) *Family therapy: An intimate history*. New York: Norton.

Home Office (2000) *Reducing domestic violence: What works?* London: Policing and Reducing Crime Unit.

Hoyt, M. (2001) *Interviews with brief therapy experts*. Philadelphia, PA: Brunner-Routledge.

Hubble, M., Duncan, B. and Miller, S. (2000) *The heart and soul of change: What works in therapy*. Washington, DC: American Psychological Association.

Hughes, D. (2007) *Attachment focused family therapy*. New York: Norton.

Johnson, S. (2003) Emotionally focused therapy: Empiricism and art. In Sexton, T., Weeks, G. and Robins, M. (Eds) *Handbook of family therapy*. New York: Brunner-Routledge, pp. 263–280.

Johnson, S. (2008) Emotionally focused couple therapy. In Gurman, A. (Ed.) *Clinical handbook of couple therapy*. New York: Guilford Press, pp. 107–137.

Jones, E. (1993) *Family systems therapy*. Chichester: John Wiley & Sons.

Jones. E. (2007) Personal communication.

Jones, E. and Asen, E. (2000) *Systemic couple therapy and depression*. London: Karnac.

Kaslow, F. (1987) *The family life of psychotherapists: Clinical implications*. New York: Haworth Press.

Kaufman, G. (1992) The mysterious disappearance of battered women in family therapists' offices: Male privilege colluding with male violence. *Journal of Marital and Family Therapy*, 18: 233–243.

Keeney, B. (1983) *The aesthetics of change*. New York: Guilford Press.

Kirschenbaum, H. and Henderson, V. (1990) *The Carl Rogers Reader*. London: Constable and Co.

Kopp, S. (1976) *The naked therapist*. San Diego, CA: EdITS Publishing.

Kopp, S. (1977) *Back to one*. Palo Alto, CA: Science and Behavior Books.

Kozlowska, K. and Hanney, L. (2001) The network perspective: An integration of attachment and family systems theories. *Family Process*, 41: 285–312.

Kuipers, E., Leff, J. and Lam, D. (1999) *Family work for schizophrenia*. London: Gaskell.

Kwee, M.G.T., Gergen, K. and Koshikawa, F. (2006) *Horizons in Buddhist psychology*. Chagrin Falls, OH: Taos Institute.

Larkin, P. (1974) *High windows*. London: Faber and Faber.

Larner, G. (2000) Towards a common ground in psychoanalysis and family therapy: On knowing not to know. *Journal of Family Therapy*, 22: 61–82.

Lebow, G. (2005) *Handbook of clinical family therapy*. Hoboken, NJ: John Wiley & Sons.

Lee, R. and Everett, C. (2004) *The integrative family therapy supervisor*. New York: Brunner-Routledge.

Leff, J., Kuipers, L., Berkowitz, R., Eberlein-Vries, R. and Sturgeon, D. (1982) A controlled trial of social intervention in families of schizophrenic patients. *British Journal of Psychiatry*, 141: 121–134.

Lerner, S. (1999) Interactions between the therapist's and client life cycle stages. In Carter, B. and McGoldrick, M, (Eds) *The expanded family life cycle*. Boston, MA: Allyn and Bacon, pp. 512–519.

Lieberman, S. (1980) *Transgenerational family therapy*. London: Croom Helm.

Lieberman, S. (1987) Going back to your own family. In Bentovim, A., Gorrell Barnes, G. and Cooklin, A. (Eds) *Family therapy: Complementary frameworks of theory and practice*. London: Academic Press, pp. 205–220.

Lieberman, S. (1995) How I assess for family therapy. In Mace, C. (Ed.) *The art and science of assessment in psychotherapy*. London: Routledge, pp. 61–77.

Loewenthal, D. and Snell, R. (2003) *Post-modernism for psychotherapists*. Hove: Brunner-Routledge.

Lowe, R. (2004) *Family therapy: A constructive framework*. London: Sage.

Lyon, D. (1994) *Postmodernity*. Buckingham: Open University Press.

Lyotard, J.-F. (1984) *The postmodern condition*. Manchester: Manchester University Press.

Mace, C. (1995) *The art and science of assessment in psychotherapy*. London: Routledge.

Madanes, C. (1981) *Strategic family therapy*. San Francisco, CA: Jossey-Bass.

May, J. (2005) Family attachment narrative therapy: Healing the experience of early childhood maltreatment. *Journal of Marital and Family Therapy*, 31: 221–238.

McGoldrick, M. and Hardy, K. (2008) *Re-visioning family therapy*. New York: Guilford Press.

McGoldrick, M., Pearce, J. and Giordano, J. (1982) *Ethnicity and family therapy*. New York: Guilford Press.

McGoldrick, M., Anderson, C. and Walsh, F. (1991) *Women in families: A framework for family therapy*. New York: Norton.

McGoldrick, M., Giordano, J. and Pearce, J. (1996) *Ethnicity and family therapy*. New York: Guilford Press.

McGoldrick, M., Gerson, R. and Shellenberger, S. (1999) *Genograms: Assessment and intervention*. New York: Norton.

McLeod, J. (1997) *Narrative and psychotherapy*. London: Sage.

McNamee, S. (2004) Promiscuity in the practice of family therapy. *Journal of Family Therapy*, 26: 224–244.

McNamee, S. (2007) Relational practices in education: Teaching as conversation. In Anderson, H. and Gehart, D. (Eds) *Collaborative therapy*. New York: Routledge, pp. 313–336.

McNamee, S. and Gergen, K. (1992) *Therapy as social construction*. London: Sage.

Miller, G. and Baldwin, D. (2000) Implications of the wounded healer paradigm for the use of self in therapy. In Baldwin, M. (Ed.) *The use of self in therapy* (2nd edn). New York: Haworth Press, pp. 243–261.

Miller, W. and Rollnick, S. (2002) *Motivational interviewing*. New York: Guilford Press.

Minuchin, P., Colapinto, J. and Minuchin, S. (1998) *Working with families of the poor*. New York: Guilford Press.

Minuchin, S. (1974) *Families and family therapy*. Cambridge, MA: Harvard University Press.

Minuchin, S. (1998) Where is the family in narrative family therapy? *Journal of Marital and Family Therapy*, 24: 397–403.

Minuchin, S. and Fishman, H.C. (1981) *Family therapy techniques*. Cambridge, MA: Harvard University Press.

Morgan, M. and Sprenkle, D. (2007) Toward a common-factors approach to supervision. *Journal of Marital and Family Therapy*, 33: 1–17.

Morton, A. (1987) Who started it? Remarks on causation. In Walrond-Skinner, S. and Watson, D. (Eds) *Ethical issues in family therapy*. London: Routledge & Kegan Paul, pp. 35–42.

Muncie, J., Wetherell, M., Langan, M., Dallos, R. and Cochrane, A. (1997) *Understanding the family*. London: Sage.

NICE (2004a) *Depression: Management of depression in primary and secondary care*. London: National Institute of Clinical Excellence.

NICE (2004b) *Eating disorders: Core interventions in the treatment and management of anorexia nervosa, bulimia nervosa and related eating disorders*. London: National Institute of Clinical Excellence.

NICE (2004c) *Self harm. The short term physical and psychological management and secondary prevention of self harm in primary and secondary care*. London: National Institute of Clinical Excellence.

NICE (2004d) *Type 1 diabetes. Diagnosis and management in children and young people*. London: National Institute of Clinical Excellence.

NICE (2005) *Obsessive compulsive disorder*. London: National Institute of Clinical Excellence.

NICE (2006) *Bipolar disorder: The management of bipolar disorder in adults, children and adolescents in primary and secondary care*. London: National Institute of Clinical Excellence.

Nichols, M. and Schwartz, R. (1998) *Family therapy: Concepts and methods*. Boston, MA: Allyn and Bacon.

Nock, S. (2000) The divorce of marriage from parenthood. *Journal of Family Therapy*, 22: 245–263.

O'Brian, C. and Bruggen, P. (1982) Our personal and professional lives: Learning positive connotation and circular questioning. *Family Process*, 24: 311–322.

O'Connor, J. and McDermott, I. (1997) *The art of systems thinking*. London: Thorsons.

O'Hagan, K. (2001) *Cultural competence in the caring professions*. London: Jessica Kingsley Publishers.

O'Leary, C. (1999) *Counselling couples and families*. London: Sage.

Olson, D. (2000) Circumplex model of marital and family systems. *Journal of Family Therapy*, 22: 144–167.

Palazzoli, M.S., Boscolo, L., Cecchin, G. and Prata, G. (1978) *Paradox and counter-paradox: A new model in the therapy of the family in schizophrenic transaction*. Northvale, NJ: Aronson.

Palazzoli, M.S., Boscolo, L., Cecchin, G. and Prata, G. (1980a) Hypothesizing, circularity, neutrality: Three guidelines for the conductor of the session. *Family Process*, 19: 3–12.

Palazzoli, M.S., Boscolo, L., Cecchin, G. and Prata, G. (1980b) The problem of the referring person. *Journal of Marital and Family Therapy*, 6: 3–9.

Payne, M. (2006) *Narrative therapy*. London: Sage.

Pearce, B. (1994) *Interpersonal communication: Making social worlds*. New York: Harper-Collins.

Pearce, B. and Cronen, V.E. (1980) *Communication, action and meaning*. New York: Praeger.

Penn, P. (1982) Circular questioning. *Family Process*, 21: 267–280.

Pilgrim, D. (1992) Psychotherapy and political evasions. In Dryden, W. and Feltham, C. (Eds) *Psychotherapy and its discontents*. Buckingham: Open University Press, pp. 225–243.

Pilgrim, D. (1997) *Psychotherapy and society*. London: Sage.

Pinsof, W.M. (1983) Integrative problem-centered therapy: Toward the synthesis of family and individual psychotherapies. *Journal of Marital and Family Therapy*, 9: 19–35.

Pinsof, W.M. (1995) *Integrative problem centered therapy*. New York: Basic Books.

Pinsof, W.M. and Wynne, L.C. (1995) The efficacy of marital and family therapy: An empirical overview, conclusions and recommendations. *Journal of Marital and Family Therapy*, 21: 585–613.

Plotkin, B. (2003) *Soulcraft*. Novato, CA: New World Library.

Pocock, D. (1995) Searching for a better story: Harnessing modern and postmodern positions in family therapy. *Journal of Family Therapy*, 17: 149–173.

Pocock, D. (2005) Systems of the heart: Evoking the feeling self in family therapy. In Flaskas, C., Mason, B. and Perlesz, A. (Eds) *The space between*. London: Karnac, pp. 127–139.

Pocock, D. (2006) Six things worth knowing about psychoanalytic psychotherapy. *Journal of Family Therapy*, 28: 352–369.

Poster, M. (1978) *The critical theory of the family*. London: Pluto Press.

Pratt, J., Gordon, P. and Plamping, D. (2005) *Working whole systems*. Oxford: Radcliffe Publishing.

Raval, H. (1996) A systemic perspective on working with interpreters. *Clinical Child Psychology and Psychiatry*, 1: 29–43.

Reimers, S. and Street, E. (1993) Using family therapy in child and adolescent services. In Carpenter, J. and Treacher, A. (Eds) *Using family therapy in the 90s*. Oxford: Blackwell, pp. 32–56.

Reimers, S. and Treacher, A. (1995) *Introducing user-friendly family therapy*. London: Routledge.

Reps, P. (1971) *Zen flesh, Zen bones*. Harmondsworth: Penguin Books.

Rivett, M. (2006) Treatment for perpetrators of domestic violence: Controversy in policy and practice. *Criminal Behaviour and Mental Health*, 16: 205–210.

Rivett, M. (2008) Metamorphosis: Towards the transformation of family therapy. *Child and Adolescent Mental Health*, 13: 102–106.

Rivett, M. and Street, E. (2001) Themes and connections of spirituality in family therapy. *Family Process*, 40: 457–465.

Rivett, M. and Street, E. (2003) *Family therapy in focus*. London: Sage.

Rivett, M. and Rees, A. (2004) Dancing on a razor's edge: Systemic group work with batterers. *Journal of Family Therapy*, 26: 142–162.

Rivett. M. and Rees, A. (2008) Working with perpetrators of domestic violence. In Green, S., Lancaster, E. and Feasey, S. (Eds) *Addressing offending behaviour*. London: Willan, pp. 344–364.

Rivett, M., Tomsett, J., Lumsdon, P. and Holmes, P. (1997) Strangers in a familiar place. *Journal of Family Therapy*, 19: 43–57.

Rivett, M., Howarth, E. and Harold, G. (2006) Watching from the stairs: Towards an evidenced based practice with child witnesses of domestic violence. *Journal of Clinical Child Psychiatry and Psychology*, 11: 103–125.

Robbins, M., Turner, C., Alexander, J. and Perez, G. (2003) Alliance and dropout in family therapy with drug using adolescents: Individual and systemic effects. *Journal of Family Psychology*, 4: 534–544.

Rober, P. (1999) The therapist's inner conversation in family therapy practice: Some ideas about the self of the therapist, therapeutic impasse, and the process of reflection. *Family Process*, 38: 209–228.

Roberts, J. (2005) Transparency and self disclosure in family therapy: Dangers and possibilities. *Family Process*, 44: 45–63.

Robinson, M. (1997) *Divorce as family transition*. London: Karnac.

Roffman, A. (2005) Function at the junction: Revisiting the idea of functionality in family therapy. *Journal of Marital and Family Therapy*, 31: 259–268.

Rogers, A. and Pilgrim, D. (2001) *Mental health policy in Britain*. Basingstoke: Palgrave.

Rose, N. (1999) *Governing the soul*. London: Free Association Press.

Roth, A. and Fonagy, P. (1996) *What works for whom? A critical view of psychotherapy research*. London: Guilford Press.

Rowe, C. and Liddle, H. (2002) Substance misuse. In Sprenkle, D. (Ed.) *Effectiveness research in marriage and family therapy*. Alexandria, VA: American Association for Marriage and Family Therapy, pp. 53–87.

Ryan, C., Epstein, N., Keitner, I. and Bishop, D. (2005) *Evaluating and treating families: The McMaster approach*. New York: Routledge.

Safran, J. and Muran, J.C. (2000) *Negotiating the therapeutic alliance*. New York: Guilford Press.

Scaife, J. (2001) *Supervision in the mental health professions*. Hove: Brunner-Routledge.

Schön, D. (1983) *The reflective practitioner*. New York: Basic Books.

Seikkula, J. (2002) Open dialogues with good and poor outcomes for psychotic cases. *Journal of Marital and Family Therapy*, 28: 263–274.

Sexton, T., Weeks, G. and Robbins, M. (2003) *Handbook of family therapy*. New York: Brunner-Routledge.

Sexton, T., Kinser, J. and Hanes, C. (2008) Beyond a single standard: Levels of evidence approach for evaluating marriage and family therapy research and practice. *Journal of Family Therapy*, 30: 386–398.

Shadley, M. (2000) Are all family therapists alike? Revisiting research about the use of self in therapy. In Baldwin, M. (Ed.) *The use of self in therapy*. New York: Haworth Press, pp. 191–212.

Sheidow, A., Henggeler, S. and Schoenwald, S. (2003) Multisystemic therapy. In Sexton, T., Weeks, G. and Robbins, M. (Eds) *Handbook of Family Therapy*. New York: Brunner-Routledge, pp. 303–322.

Siegal, R. (2007) *The mindful brain*. New York: Norton.

Silverstein, O. and Rashbaum, B. (1994) *The courage to raise good men*. New York: Penguin.

Simon, G. (1992) Having second order mind while doing first order therapy. *Journal of Marital and Family Therapy*, 18: 377–387.

Simon, R. (1989) Family life cycle issues in the therapy system. In Carter, B. and McGoldrick, M. (Eds) *The changing family life cycle*. Boston, MA: Allyn and Bacon, pp. 107–117.

Skynner, R. (1976) *One flesh, separate persons*. London: Constable.

Speed, B. (2004) All aboard in the NHS: Collaborating with colleagues who use different approaches. *Journal of Family Therapy*, 26: 260–279.

Sprenkle, D. (2002) *Effectiveness research in marriage and family therapy*. Alexandria, VA: American Association for Marriage and Family Therapy.

Steinglas, P. (2009) Systemic-motivational therapy for substance abuse disorders: An integrative model. *Journal of Family Therapy*, 31: 155–174.

Street, E. (1989) Challenging the white knight. In Dryden, W. and Spurling, L. (Eds) *On becoming a psychotherapist*. London: Routledge, pp. 134–147.

Street, E. (1994) *Counselling for family problems*. London: Sage.

Street, E. and Downey, J. (1996) *Brief therapeutic consultations*. London: John Wiley & Sons.

Street, E. and Rivett, M. (1996) Stress and coping in the practice of family therapy. *Journal of Family Therapy*, 18: 303–319.

Street, E. and Dryden, W. (1988) *Family therapy in Britain*. Milton Keynes: Open University Press.

Sulloway, F. (1997) *Born to rebel*. New York: Vintage.

Tomm, K. (1988) Interventive interviewing: Intending to ask lineal, circular, strategic or reflexive questions? *Family Process*, 27: 1–15.

Treacher, A. (1989) Termination in family therapy – developing a structural approach. *Journal of Family Therapy*, 11: 135–148.

Treacher, A. and Carpenter, J. (1984) *Using family therapy*. Oxford: Blackwell.

Turnell. A. and Essex, S. (2006) *Working with denied child abuse*. Maidenhead: Open University Press.

Varma, V. (1997) *Stress in psychotherapists*. London: Routledge.

Vetere, A. and Dallos, R. (2008) Systemic therapy and attachment narratives. *Journal of Family Therapy*, 30: 374–385.

Walker, S. and Akister, J. (2004) *Applying family therapy*. Lyme Regis: Russell House Publishing.

Walrond-Skinner, S. (1976) *Family therapy*. London: Routledge & Kegan Paul.

Walrond-Skinner, S. (1998) The function and role of forgiveness in working with couples and families. *Journal of Family Therapy*, 20: 3–20.

Walsh, F. (1998) *Strengthening family resilience*. New York: Guilford Press.

Walsh, F. (1999) *Spiritual resources in family therapy*. New York: Guilford Press.

Walsh, F. (2003) *Normal family processes*. New York: Guilford Press.

Walters, M. (1990) A feminist perspective in family therapy. In

Perelberg, R. and Miller, A. (Eds) *Gender and power in families.* London: Routledge, pp. 13–33.

Watzlawick, P., Weakland, J. and Fisch, R. (1974) *Change: Principles of problem formation and problem resolution.* New York: Norton.

Welwood, J. (2000) *Toward a psychology of awakening.* London. Shambala.

White, M. (1995) *Re-authoring lives.* Adelaide: Dulwich Centre Publications.

White, M. (2007) *Maps of narrative practice.* New York: Norton.

White, M. and Epston, D. (1990) *Narrative means to therapeutic ends.* New York: Norton.

Williams, P. (2009) *Mahayana Buddhism* (2nd edn). London: Routledge.

Wilson, J. (1998) *Child focused practice.* London: Karnac.

Woodcock, J. (2001) Threads from the labyrinth. *Journal of Family Therapy*, 23: 136–154.

Wynne, L., McDaniel, S. and Weber, T. (1986) *Systems consultation.* New York: Guilford Press.

Zeig, J. (2001) *Changing directives: The strategic therapy of Jay Haley.* Phoenix, AZ: Milton Erickson Foundation Press.